WORKING LIVES

The Railway Industry

Betty Williams

B T BATSFORD LTD   LONDON

Typeset by Tek-Art Ltd, Kent
and printed in Great Britain by
R.J. Acford Ltd,
Chichester, Sussex
for the publishers
B.T. Batsford Ltd,
4 Fitzhardinge Street,
London W1H 0AH

ISBN 0 7134 5539 X

Frontispiece
Track re-laying near Crewe in 1986 (Tina Coates).

Cover illustrations
*The colour photograph shows relief leading railman
Steve Allen collecting tickets at Stratford station, 1987*
(Tina Coates); *the black and white print shows staff at
Clapham Junction station, 1889* (National Railway
Museum); *the portrait is of driver Frankie McCardle in
the cab of an LNER locomotive* (L.A. Fairburn).

Acknowledgments
The Author and Publishers would like to thank the
following for their kind permission to reproduce
illustrations and extracts: Beamish North of England
Open Air Museum for figures 16 and 17 and for extracts
from Miles Dent's journals; British Rail Youth Training
Scheme, Newcastle, for figure 49; British Railways
Board for figure 50; Derek Cornforth for figure 31 and
for extracts from the Darlington general strike log; L.A.
Fairbairn for figures 28 and 34; R. Hooker for figure 48;
David Lovering for figure 26; Mansell Collection for
figures 7, 11, 12, 13 and 18; National Museum of Labour
History for figures 19 and 20; National Railway Museum
for figures 10, 15, 22, 25 and 29; National Union of
Railwaymen for figure 24; *Newcastle Evening
Chronicle* for figures 39 and 42; Science Museum for
figures 2, 3 and 6; T.E. Smith for figures 35, 36, 41 and 43;
Neville Stead for figures 23 and 37. Figures 4, 5, 8, 14,
21, 27 and 32 are from the Publishers collection.
Figures 1, 9, 38, 40, 44, 45, 46 and 47 were photographed
by Tina Coates.

The Author is grateful for help received from British
Rail, Coventry Area Manager John Brazier and Rugby
Traffic Manager Peter Hunt; the NUR; ASLEF; the
Newcastle drivers' LDC and T.E. Smith; and to the
Public Record Office and British Railways Board for
access to British Transport Historical Records. Very
special thanks go to all the railway men and women
who agreed to be interviewed and whose names
appear in the book.

Contents

List of Illustrations

Introduction

The train now arriving at Platform 2 is the 9.43 for London King's Cross, calling at Darlington, York, Peterborough . . .

Thousands of announcements like this are made all over the country every day, yet how many of the passengers hurrying to get a seat stop to think of all the complicated manoeuvres which make it possible for that train to arrive at that station at that time? How many know anything about the working lives of the people involved in the daily operation of Britain's railway system?

A hundred years ago a railway historian, Sir William Acworth, dedicated a book to the 'Servants of the Public who are at work by night as well as by day, in fog as well as in sunshine, upon the Railways of England'. The dedication was unusual then because far more was written about famous engines and different railway lines than about the men who worked on them. It would also be unusual today, when books about locomotives and railway construction and company histories are still numerous but comparatively little is ever put on paper about the railway workers.

'People don't understand what we do' says driver's assistant, Paul James, at Waterloo. 'The passengers are just using it as transport,' says Andrew Hall, who went on a BR youth training scheme at Newcastle. 'They only see the guard on the train, the booking clerk and the ticket collector. They don't know what goes on behind the scenes.'

It is over 150 years since Robert Stephenson's *Rocket* astonished the world with a speed of 29 miles an hour. Now, British Rail's high speed locomotives can travel up to 140 m.p.h., twice the speed allowed to cars on motorways. Yet the routes built by the great Victorian engineers remain. 'Down' trains from London to Glasgow still plunge into the Kilsby tunnel constructed by Robert Stephenson on his London & Birmingham

---

1 *Drivers' assistant Paul James – 'People ask me "Do you steer it?" '*

line in 1838; 'up' trains from Cornwall to London still cross the river Tamar into Devon over Brunel's Royal Albert Bridge.

Railway traditions go back a long way. Steam trains had vanished by the 1960s, yet many drivers still call the second man in the cab the 'fireman'; it is well over a hundred years since railway policemen directed trains by hand-signals like a 'traffic cop' on the roads, yet a signalman operating electronic power controls is still referred to as the 'bobby'.

These traditions stem from ways of working and events in railway history about which passengers 'just using it as transport' know little. What was it like to be a driver or a station master in the nineteenth century? What did a porter do in the 1920s, or a platelayer in the 1950s? What is the job like today and how much has it changed?

To find out, let us go 'behind the scenes'.

1 The Pioneers

The first railway waggons were pulled by horses. In coal-mining areas, especially in the North-East of England, trucks known as chaldrons were fitted on to wooden rails to carry loads of coal to canals and rivers. Horses, treading between the tracks, pulled them back up to the pithead.

These tramways were used only by the mines to which they belonged, but in 1803 a line with iron rails was opened on which anyone could pay to send their goods. It was called the Surrey Iron Railway and ran from Wandsworth on the Thames in London to the town of Croydon.

A year later a steam locomotive was driven along a railway track under its own power. This momentous occasion took place at Penydarren in South Wales and the man responsible was a Cornish engineer called Richard Trevithick. Many engineers experimented with 'motive power' but the man who became known as the 'Father of Railways' was George Stephenson, who was born in Northumberland in 1781 and started work at the age of eight driving cattle off a colliery

---

2 *The opening of the Stockton & Darlington Railway.*

tramway. Later he went down the pit, but also began building engines for his employers at Killingworth colliery.

The Stockton & Darlington Railway

In 1821 a Quaker industrialist, Edward Pease, decided to build a railway to take coal from the Durham pits for shipment to London by sea. Stephenson was chosen as chief engineer of the project and he made his son, Robert, his assistant. Between them they not only constructed the line but also built its locomotives.

There was immense excitement when the Stockton & Darlington Railway was opened in

1825 with George Stephenson at the controls of his No. 1 engine, *Locomotion*. He drove it at speeds reaching 15 m.p.h. to Stockton-on-Tees where the train was greeted by a 21-gun-salute – a fitting tribute for the dawn of the Railway Age.

Drivers

The Stockton & Darlington line was built for goods traffic but a surprising number of passengers also wanted to travel by rail. At first horses as well as locomotives were used and special sidings were provided on the track so that they could pull in to let the faster 'iron horses' pass. Often the horse-drivers refused to give way and there was an unceasing war between drivers of old and new.

John Graham was the first traffic manager of the line. His son, George, became an engine driver and years later he recorded some of the things his father had told him about the railway's early days. His notes are now in the British Transport Historical Records collection at the Public Record Office, Kew.

Eight miles an hour was the maximum speed allowed and the engine drivers were often in trouble for going too fast. One man was dismissed for 'excess speed' and another fined £1 for driving at 12 m.p.h. downhill. The early engines had no brakes and no reversing gear. To pull up, the driver had to manipulate the pistons and connecting rods.

. . . the driver had to work his handles in the opposite direction to what the engine was running and this often on a falling gradient which meant the working of the handles four times for every revolution of the wheels . . . . I have heard it said that there was only one driver who could manage this in the dark without a light, named William Chicken.

Graham described Chicken as 'a very active man' who 'was often reported for running at too high a speed, thereby causing the cast iron wheels of the waggons to break'. He later became a driver of 'express' trains in Scotland.

3   *The Olive Mount cutting on the Liverpool & Manchester Railway.*

Most of the early drivers were 'rather spreeish characters', Graham remembered.

When a lad of seven years of age, I had my attention drawn into a public house ... where a lot of drivers were on the spree and they actually had their watches in a frying pan on the fire.

They were not only 'spreeish', but tough. They had to be, for as writer L.T.C. Rolt puts it:

With unbelievably primitive machines and equipment and with no precedents whatever to guide them, they had to learn by bitter trial and error how to run a railway.
(*George and Robert Stephenson*)

The *Rocket*

The first railway to be worked entirely by steam engines was the Liverpool & Manchester Railway. It too was constructed by George Stephenson who not only had to cut through a wall of rock outside Liverpool and build a viaduct to carry the line over a wide valley, but also had to lay the tracks across a treacherous bog called Chat Moss.

Robert Stephenson's *Rocket* won the Rainhill Trials held in 1829 to decide whose engines should be bought for the new line. It was the *Rocket*, driven by another engineer, Joseph Locke, which ran over William Huskisson MP at the opening ceremony in 1830. He died later that night, so achieving the dubious distinction of becoming the first passenger to be killed in a railway accident.

Brunel

Robert Stephenson became the engineer of the London & Birmingham Railway which opened in 1838. It joined up with Locke's Grand Junction Railway, completed the year before between Birmingham and Manchester. Further south, another great engineer, Isambard Kingdom Brunel, was building the Great Western Railway, the first stretch of which, from London to Bristol, was opened in 1838.

Brunel's achievements range from railways to

---

4   *The 'Break of Gauge' at Gloucester: a contemporary illustration.*

steamships and include engineering feats such as the Box Tunnel, near Bath, and the Clifton Suspension Bridge at Bristol. Though Stephenson had fixed his gauge – the distance between rails – at 4 ft 8½ in., which was the same as the colliery tramways, Brunel decided that a broad gauge of 7 ft ¼ in. would give a safer and more comfortable ride.

Other railways copied Stephenson and in 1846 the narrower gauge became standard to all except the GWR. This meant a 'break of gauge'

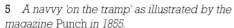

5   A navvy 'on the tramp' as illustrated by the magazine Punch *in 1855.*

whenever the GWR met other companies' lines, with passengers and freight transferring to different carriages and waggons. Complaints were loud and crises frequent. The magazine *Punch* told the story of a woman laden with parcels who panicked as the train pulled out – she had left her baby 'on the ledge at Gloster'.

Navvies

Engineers were the pioneers in railway development, but it was the navvies who actually built the lines. They got their name from the 'navigators' who constructed canals in the eighteenth century. At the peak of railway building in Britain there were about 200,000 of them moving 'on the tramp' from job to job, living usually in makeshift shanty towns beside the track and often putting rural communities into a turmoil of fright by their riotous behaviour. Though navvies' wages were higher than those of farm workers, their hours were often longer and their conditions much worse. The contractors usually paid them only once a month, distributing the money in public houses so that they spent a lot of it on drink. Until next pay day they lived 'on truck', taking tickets from the contractor for a 'tommy shop' on the site which sold food and clothes at prices far higher than an ordinary shop.

Navvying in the 1840s was described to writer A.R. Tregelles by a Wiltshire navvy's wife:

'Twas wintertime coming, and they was working nothing but muck. Charley was tipping then . . . and 'tis dreadful hard to get the stuff out of the wagons when 'tis streaming wet atop and all stodge under. Then, you see, he was standing in it over his boots all day long; and once – no, twice – when he draw'd out his foot, the sole of his boot was left in the dirt . . . . One Saturday night he took out his back money, and said us wid tramp for Yorkshire . . . .
(*The Ways of the Line*)

Gunpowder was used to blast a way through rock surfaces but after that the work had to be carried out with only picks, shovels and wheelbarrows. 'Barrow runs' of planks were placed up the sides of excavations and the navvy would 'make the running' up the steep walls balancing his barrow, laden with earth and stones, in front of him. Those who tripped were often badly injured or killed.

Thirty-two navvies were killed and 700 injured during the six years it took to construct the Woodhead tunnel in Cheshire. It was driven for three miles at a depth of 200 metres beneath the rock and shale of the Pennines.

Few monuments were put up to the navvies who lost their lives building the railways. Their true memorials, however, are the deep tunnels and long cuttings through which our modern trains still travel.

Railway Mania

The last major line to be built by navvies was the Settle & Carlisle in 1875, but nearly all the main trunk routes were completed by mid-century. Two great spurts of building in the 1830s and 1840s were dubbed the 'Railway Mania'. By 1851 Britain had more than 6000 miles of line.

Railways caused immense changes. Not only coal, but goods of all kinds were transported further and faster. Fish trains were run from the ports; newspaper trains left London in the small hours; milk churns were picked up at rural stations; and mail was distributed all over the country.

The nineteenth-century railways were a self-contained industry. Their main stations were often architectural marvels and next to them were built equally imposing hotels for the passengers' use. The railways also ran the steamship services which took them across the Channel or to Ireland. They put up rows of houses for their workers to live in and often provided their children with schools. They built their own locomotives and rolling stock and whole towns such as Swindon in Wiltshire and Crewe in Cheshire grew up around their engineering workshops. In his book *Stokers*

and Pokers, published in 1849, Sir Francis Head described Wolverton on the London & North Western Railway:

... a little red-brick town composed of 242 little red-brick houses ... three or four tall red-brick engine chimneys, a number of very large red-brick workshops, six red-brick houses for officers – one red beer shop, two red public-houses ... a substantial red school-room and a neat stone church, the whole lately built by order of a Railway Board, at a railway station, by a railway contractor, for railway men, railway women, and railway children; in short, the round cast-iron plate over the door of every house, bearing the letters L.N.W.R. is the generic symbol of the town.

6 *North Eastern Railway announcement of a special 'Fish Train' in 1864.*

7 *The contrast between first and third class was still great in 1892, as these pictures show. The Midland Railway abolished second class in 1872 and eventually other companies did the same. It was not until after the Second World War that third class was renamed second.*

Passengers

At first there were three classes of passenger carriage, with accommodation varying from the luxury of first class to bare wooden seats for those with third-class tickets. Some companies were reluctant to provide third-class carriages at all because they did not make big enough profits, but in 1844 Gladstone's Government passed a Railway Act which laid down that on all lines there should be at least one train a day with fares of 1d a mile or less and a speed of at least 12 m.p.h. These 'workmen's trains' became known to railwaymen as 'Parliamentaries'.

Trains had no heating, though passengers could hire metal foot-warmers, and only dim oil lights. There were no corridors, no lavatories and no refreshment cars. The GWR allowed passengers from London ten minutes in the station refreshment room at Swindon before their train left on its seven-and-a-half hour journey to Cornwall.

Railway catering was mocked as much then as it is now. The novelist Charles Dickens singled out for attack the refreshment room at Rugby, which he called 'Mugby'. In *The Uncommercial Traveller*, published in 1860, he complained:

I cannot dine on stale sponge-cakes that turn to sand in the mouth. I cannot dine on shining brown patties, composed of unknown animals within . . . .

2 Jobs on the Victorian Railway

The railway industry very soon became a big new source of work. In 1850 it employed 60,000 people, but by the 1870s this had risen to 275,000. There were scores of different jobs.

Station staff

Even quite small Victorian stations teemed with staff, from the head porter down to the humble lamp boy who cleaned the station oil lamps. In charge was the station master who usually had a house adjoining the station and was on call at all times. He was a person of some note in the community.

Ernest Simmons was station master at Thame on the GWR in the 1850s:

I reigned almost supreme . . . . As I went to and from my house to the station the little boys in the street used to say 'That's the Station Master', and on Sunday quite a tribe of country people walked in to see the trains start . . . .

8 *Staff at Lewes station in Sussex in the 1870s. Note the station master in his top hat.*

When he was promoted to Bilston in Staffordshire he had a staff of six clerks, 35 men and 12 horses.

My attention was fully taken up by starting trains, opening quite 300 business letters daily, collecting 80 ledger accounts monthly, canvassing for traffic in opposition to the Long and Narrow Railway [LNWR], checking and balancing all accounts and . . . on the general business of the station.
(*Ernest Struggles*)

The station master's salary was based on the amount of traffic through his station. In the 1860s the salary range was between £50 and £250 a year. At Thame Ernest Simmons got £80 and paid £8 a year rent for his house.

Though a station master at a large London terminus such as Paddington or Euston would be in charge of hundreds of employees and responsible for dozens of trains each hour, every station, however small, had its station master. In some cases he was the only person there. In 1857 the Great Northern Railway increased the pay of the station master at Manston and Cross Gates in Yorkshire from 18s to 20s a week 'in consideration of his wife having to attend to the gates at the level crossing at Manston Station during his absence at Cross Gates'.

Clerks

Under the station master the railways employed a series of clerks graded from head clerk through booking-office clerk and goods clerk to lad clerk. The average salary of clerks on the London Brighton & South Coast Railway in 1871 was £55 a year but top clerks at a company head office could earn more than many station masters.

At first a ticket for each passenger was laboriously written out by hand, but in 1837 Thomas Edmondson, a booking clerk on the Newcastle & Carlisle Railway, devised a system of cardboard tickets already printed with destination and fare category. They were stored in a specially designed rack and taken out to be date-stamped by machine. Edmondson's system, though rapidly being replaced by computerized tickets, is still in use at many stations today.

Railway boundaries were clearly defined and jealously guarded, but passengers could buy 'through' tickets which took them to their destinations over the rails of several different companies. A Railway Clearing House was set up to deal with joint matters such as this.

9   *Booking clerk Mervyn Dearlove stands beside an Edmondson ticket rack at Rugby Station in 1986.*

Enginemen

10 *Inside a Midland Railway locomotive cab.*

Drivers regarded themselves as 'Kings of the Road' and to become one meant a hard climb up the steps of a clearly defined ladder of promotion. The progress started when a boy became an engine cleaner in the running shed where locomotives were prepared for the 'road'. Then, as a 'passed cleaner' he took on fireman's duties when needed until eventually he became a full fireman.

Michael Reynolds, a Victorian engineer who styled himself 'The Engine-Driver's Friend' described the fireman's first job like this:

On the shunting engine the young fireman learns to handle the brake, so as to bring the engine up to the waggons without loss of time, and without damaging them. He learns also, in a limited way, how to handle the shovel; how to put an injector 'on' and 'off', and he acquires a bit of knowledge respecting coupling up [linking carriages] . . . . After a fireman has been engaged in forming trains, and has learnt to distinguish signals, and to ply the shovel pretty freely, he is promoted to the platform of a goods-engine – the pick-up goods – running from station to station, setting 'off' and picking 'up' waggons . . . . By shunting at different places for the passenger trains and express goods, he learns the position of signals, the road, and the traffic . . . eighteen or twenty hours a day on duty have been a very common occurrence, on an engine without any weather-board, and with wet sand-boxes, and in all sorts of hard weather . . . but they have been buoyed up with the thought that their passenger days were ahead.

(*Engine-driving Life, 1881*)

On slow goods trains out in the country, driver and fireman could sometimes have a fairly easy existence. There are tales of enginemen picking lineside flowers, doing a bit of poaching and frying bacon on the shovel. On fast passenger trains, however, especially as engines got heavier and more powerful, the work for both was arduous.

The fireman had to break up the coal in the tender and then, standing on the swaying, lurching footplate, often in lashing rain, high winds or snow, during a shift lasting 12 hours or more, shovel up to six tons of coal through the narrow door of the firebox. And it could not be thrown in just anyhow. He had to 'flash the blade', which meant, as G.E. Mitton put it in 1909,

. . . to spread his coal evenly in the furnace with just that dexterous sweep that nothing but long practice can give, so that the fire may be glowing in every part, and not black in places and thin in others. He must be firing up constantly, so as to keep the pressure of steam even. . . . He has also to regulate the supply of water from the tank to the boiler . . . and when not otherwise engaged he has to assist the driver in keeping a lookout.
(*The Book of the Railway*)

The next rung on the ladder was 'passed fireman' which denoted a fireman who had passed tests enabling him to drive engines when required. Then, as a full driver, he would once more go through the sequence of shunting engines, goods trains and slow passenger trains before becoming at long last – and the process could take twenty years or more – a driver of express passenger locomotives.

The driver was in charge of the engine and of the fireman – and his word was law. In the 1870s top drivers earned 7s 6d a day; firemen were paid around 5s. Drivers were organized, as they still are, in 'links' – groups of men doing the same driving jobs in rotation. 'Top link' drivers took the express passenger trains.

When George Graham started driving, railways were so new that it was possible for a driver to take a train over 'roads' which were unknown to him. In 1844 he was sent to Derby to collect four locomotives for the Stockton & Darlington.

We left Derby at 4 a.m. with steam up on one engine, and hauling the other three . . . . We did not know one yard of the line, or any signals

between Clay Cross and Darlington . . . . When we got to Altofts Junction instead of keeping the line to York, we went towards Leeds and we had travelled a few miles in that direction before we found out our mistake, and then we had to shunt back . . . . We arrived at Shildon at 10 p.m. I have never been so tired and knocked up since . . .
(From notes in the British Transport Historical Records collection)

Soon, however, with more lines and increased traffic, drivers had to 'learn the road' – its signals, stations, junctions and gradients, before taking out a train.

Guards

The third member of the train crew was the guard. He had to start the train according to the timetable by giving the driver the 'right away' by whistle or green flag, and on the journey had to

---

11 *A guard on the London & North Western Railway blows his whistle to give the train the 'Right Away'.*

look after the passengers and parcels, or freight. He was an essential link in the train's braking system – and in the early days this was primitive. On goods trains he had to leap along the tops of the waggons to pull on their hand-brakes individually. The brake in the guard's van had to be applied when the engine was stopping or going downhill, the driver keeping in touch by a series of blasts on the locomotive's whistle.

The railway companies were reluctant to spend money on braking systems but by the 1860s 'continuous' brakes, which operated all along the train, were being developed. They did not work, though, on carriages or waggons which became uncoupled from the main part of the train. In 1889 80 people, most of them children, were killed in an accident at Armagh, in Ireland, when an excursion train broke in half and the runaway carriages hurtled into another train behind. Afterwards Parliament passed the Regulation of Railways Act which made it compulsory for railway companies to fit continuous brakes which would come on automatically if a train became divided.

12 *A signalman at London Bridge on the South-Eastern Railway in 1866 pulls a lever forward into the 'reverse' position to set a signal to allow a train to proceed.*

Signalmen

From the start it was obvious that it would be dangerous for trains to run without some form of track control. At first they were despatched on the 'time interval' system, one following the other after a few minutes' wait. If one train broke down on a single line there was nothing to stop the next one crashing into it, so under the 'block system' the line was divided into short sections with a signalbox, or block post, at each end. Under 'absolute block' only one train was allowed into a section at a time. A signalman could not accept a second train for his section until the next box had notified him that the line was clear. Boxes communicated by a system of bell codes and block telegraph instruments. For double safety on single-line sections the driver had to carry a staff, rather like the baton in a relay race, which

he handed in at the end of the section. An electrically operated apparatus from which he took a tablet, or token, was later developed.

The railway companies had – and still have – their own police forces and the first trains were directed by railway policemen giving signals by hand or with flags. Later, fixed signal posts were put up with wooden 'arms' to regulate trains on the semaphore system. Soon these were connected by rods and wires to a row of levers in the signalbox. Points, which switched trains from one track to another, were also controlled from the box and were interlocked with the signals so that the two could not conflict. At large junctions with many lines signals were placed across the tracks on a gantry.

Being a 'bobby', as signalmen were nicknamed, was lonely and carried a high degree of responsibility. It was especially difficult in bad weather conditions such as fog, when drivers could not see the signals and had to be warned of dangers by detonators placed to explode on the line.

From 1840 Government officers belonging to a special railway inspectorate at the Board of Trade carried out thorough inquiries into railway accidents. Their reports usually resulted in new safety measures.

An important change in signalling practice followed a crash in icy weather at Abbots Ripton on the Great Northern line in 1876. The accident was caused because the signal arms were frozen in the 'clear' position despite the signalman's attempts to change them to 'danger' before the 'Scotch express' thundered up the line into the back of a goods train. Henceforth, it was decided,

13 *Searching for wreckage after the Tay Bridge disaster. The engine was recovered and put back into service by the North British Railway – but for many years no driver would take it across the rebuilt bridge.*

the normal position of all signals should be at 'danger' rather than 'clear'.

Three years later the Tay Bridge disaster was blamed on the poor construction of the bridge which collapsed during a storm, sending a train with 75 passengers plunging into the icy waters of the Firth of Tay.

Trackmen

The men who looked after the track, the platelayers, or lengthmen, were in many ways the forgotten men of railways. Their work was vital in guarding against accidents yet it was seldom noticed by the travelling public.

The first rails were made with a rim like a plate – hence the term 'platelayer' – but before long the rails were flat and the wheels had flanges to stop them falling off. The standard length of rail was 60 ft. Sections were bolted together by 'fishplates' which rested on iron supports called 'chairs'. These were fixed to wooden sleepers set in a bed of small stones called ballast.

Train crew called the line the 'road' but to platelayers it was the 'permanent way'. Each line was divided into districts of about 25 miles and then subdivided into lengths of one or two miles under a ganger and two or three lengthmen. Every day they had to walk the line, checking the bolts and sleepers and repairing any faults. Teams which put down new track were known as re-laying gangs.

A permanent-way ganger in the late nineteenth century was paid 3s 9d a day, and 1s for walking his length on Sunday. His men received 3s a day. Apart from attending to the track, they trimmed the lineside trees and hedges, cut the grass and cleared the drains. They had to work during fog and snow, keeping points clear of ice and water cranes working so that engines could fill their boilers *en route*. It was a dangerous job and many platelayers were knocked down and killed through not having an adequate look-out system to warn them of approaching trains.

The end of the broad gauge

An immense operation carried out on the track was the conversion of the broad gauge to the standard width. The GWR brought 4000 of their platelayers to do the job on the remaining 127 miles of broad track, over one weekend in 1892.

The men were billeted in gangs of about sixty ... in the goods sheds, waiting rooms, and other offices, or in tents erected for the purpose along the line. Each man had a straw mattress for a bed and two rugs provided by the company; and on arrival at the allotted posts hot gruel [oatmeal and water] was served out ...
(G.A. Sekon, *A History of the Great Western Railway, 1895*)

Passengers lamented the disappearance of the comfortable broad carriages, and *Punch* published a cartoon showing the ghost of Brunel. An epitaph was chalked on a sleeper by a West Country platelayer: 'Good-bye poor old Broad Gauge. God bless you.'

3 Working Conditions

Victorian railways were organized on military lines and many of the first railway 'officers' were former army men. Railway workers were known as 'railway servants' and were expected to give themselves almost body and soul for the Company. They had to live close to their work and were awoken by the sound of a railway 'knocker up' tapping on their bedroom windows. They could be kept on duty, or called out again, at any time and especially for extra work in fog or snow.

From the beginning, railways were run on regulations and records. A rudimentary knowledge of reading, writing and arithmetic was essential, though Britain did not have compulsory education for all until 1880. Guards, for example, had to record details of waggon loads, parcels and mail bags, list arrival and departure times at stations, give reasons for delays and also make reports on weather conditions; signalmen kept log books, occurrence books and train register books.

Everyone was issued with a company *Rule Book* which became known as the railwayman's Bible. It had to be learnt thoroughly, for it covered every eventuality from standard procedures to action in emergencies. Some companies even made rules governing off-duty hours. Rule 26 in the Taff Vale Railway *Rule Book* of 1855 stated:

It is urgently required that every person . . . on Sundays and other Holy Days, when he is not required on duty, will attend a place of worship . . . .

Timekeeping

Many of the early railway workers had previously

14 *Railway companies advertised new or improved services like this, as well as publishing their own timetables. Competition for passengers was fierce, especially where two lines covered the same part of the country.*

been farm labourers and had been brought up in rural communities where their lives had been regulated by the rising and setting of the sun. But railways ran for 24 hours a day and the bulk of the goods traffic was moved in the hours of darkness. Railway work had to be organized on round-the-clock shifts.

Everything was done to time and in accordance with a timetable. Passenger timetables, such as the commercially produced *Bradshaw's Guide*, were complicated enough, but railway companies had their own working timetables which showed in far more detail all the times, such as those scheduled for various points on the route, which were essential for the smooth running of a train service.

Guards, and sometimes drivers, were issued with company watches and the station and signal-box clocks were important items which had to be time-checked daily. Greenwich Mean Time was known to many as 'Railway Time' because until the 1880s most towns kept 'local time'. Clocks in Bath and Bristol, for example, were 11 minutes behind the 'Railway Time' used by the GWR.

---

15   The Manor House disaster.

Discipline

Railway discipline in the form of reprimands, fines, suspension from duty and instant dismissal, was harsh. On the London & North Western Railway in the 1850s a man could be dismissed not only for 'incompetency' and 'intoxication' but also for 'improper language, cursing or swearing'. On the Highland Railway a man could lose his job for poor engine cleaning.

Instant dismissal was usually the penalty for any form of negligence but in addition the culprit could face prosecution in the ordinary court. Drivers or signalmen thought responsible for fatal accidents were charged with manslaughter and, if found guilty, often sentenced to several months' hard labour.

Public sympathy was aroused in the case of James Holmes, a signalman who was charged with manslaughter at York Assizes in 1892. Holmes had been up all night with his seriously ill child and spent much of the following day searching for a doctor. He returned home to find the child dead and his wife in a state of collapse. He asked to be let off as unfit for duty that night but a replacement could not be found so he started his shift at Manor House box, near Thirsk. For a

few vital minutes he fell asleep, allowing the 'Scotch express' to run into a goods train, killing eight passengers and injuring 39. He was found guilty of the offence but, to the cheers of people in court, the judge discharged him.

Despite the danger of dismissal, railway work was more secure than most jobs. Once in, it could be a job for life. Railway service soon began to run in families with father putting in a word for son and brother following brother. When jobs were scarce it was difficult to join the railways without either a family connection or some form of patronage such as a recommendation from the station master or one of the directors. Job applicants often had to have a reference also from someone of standing like the local schoolmaster or vicar.

Rivalry between the companies was very strong and so was staff loyalty, which was fostered by all sorts of concessions given to supplement wages. Some workers, such as signalmen and crossing gate-keepers, lived in company houses;

porters on the LB & SCR in the 1830s received 21s a week 'with fire and candle found'; many others had free or reduced-price coal and station masters on the NER were allowed to set up as coal merchants on the side.

Uniforms

Uniforms were provided in the company livery and re-issued at intervals. Most grades had two pairs of boots and trousers a year, though overcoats were issued only every two or three years. Guards on the S & D wore scarlet coats and porters in the early days of the GWR had top hats. This company's cattle-truck washers got oilskin leggings once a year and the station master at Paddington had a new silk hat every six months. On the North Western line in 1847 the station master had to make a daily inspection of staff to ensure that they were 'clean in their persons and clothes, shaved, and with their shoes brushed'. Great care was taken with uniform details. On the NER a station master's 'First Class Frock Coat Suit' had to be made of 'Black Vienna Cloth weighing 21 ounces to the yard, the cuffs edged with oak

16 *A group of NER staff.*

leaf braid and lined in striped sateen'. A porter's jacket was of 'Blued olive cord' with sleeve linings of 'strong unbleached calico'.

Accident and Injury

Accidents, often resulting in death, were an ever-present reality for most Victorian railwaymen. They were caused by faulty equipment, inadequate safety provisions, carelessness, or the kind of dangerous manoeuvres which had to be carried out, for example, by shunters. Shunters worked in crowded marshalling yards or goods sidings where trucks had to be uncoupled, shunted into new positions and coupled up again, often to moving trains. Most of their work was at night in narrow spaces which were badly lit.

I remember a case of a siding lit only by an old paraffin lamp placed upon the top of a pole just level with a man's face . . . . One night a shunter, in trying to utilise what little light it gave, stepped under his train and had both legs cut off. For two hours that man lay in the snow, quite conscious and suffering agonies, fingering his bloody stumps and speculating as to the future of his children when he was dead. A mate of mine was fireman on the engine at the time and all the while they were waiting for the ambulance to arrive he sat there in the snow, wrapping his own coat round the injured man, easing his thirst by putting snow into his mouth, and telling him lies as to how soon he would be out of hospital. After the inquest a mate of the deceased measured the place up and found that the radius of the light shed by the lamp was four yards . . .
(Rowland Kenney, *Men and Rails*, 1913)

Until 1880 employers were not legally liable to pay compensation for injury or death but many railway companies paid funeral expenses for their workers and also sponsored Friendly Societies which paid out small sums of money to men off work through illness or injury.

Hours of work

Many accidents were caused by the long hours

the men had to work and throughout the nineteenth century railwaymen complained about this. Until the 1860s they did a seven-day week and though pay was based on a 12-hour turn of duty, compulsory overtime, often poorly paid or not paid at all, frequently meant a working day of 20 hours or more. A guard at Leeds protested when told to take a train to London after an 18-hour stint of duty. He was told: 'You've got 24 hours in a day like every other man, and they are all ours if we want you to work them.'

Even though it was realized that these long shifts endangered the passengers as well as wearing out the railway workers, little was done about it. The medical journal, *The Lancet*, commented in 1861:

The worn out engine driver nods, and a hundred lives are in jeopardy; the signalman, dazed by want of sleep, becomes confused, and in a moment the engines are pounding up human beings between them . . . .

In that year a signalman's mistake caused a collision in Clayton Tunnel on the LB & SC line, in which 21 people were killed. At the inquiry it was discovered that the signalman had been on duty for 24 hours instead of his normal 18!

During a Royal Commission on Railway Accidents held in 1877 evidence was given of a driver who had been on duty for 40 hours without a break, and another witness said that after being on his feet for 30 or 40 hours 'I am sure I fell off the box, where I stand, asleep. I could not see the signals.'

Guard's notebook

By the 1870s railway workers were pressing for a ten-hour day but even at the turn of the century far longer hours were worked by most grades. Miles Dent, a goods guard at Waskerley and Burn Hill stations in County Durham, kept meticulous notebooks of his hours, wages and benefit-society contributions. Six of the little maroon volumes, for the years spanning 1889–1908, are now in the Beamish North of England Open Air Museum at Stanley. They show that his average hours were between 12 and 13 a day, with

17 *A train snowed up at Rowley Station on the line worked by Miles Dent. Until 1867 the village was known as Cold Rowley – and it certainly lives up to its reputation here.*

18 *Digging out a stranded locomotive during the 'Great Snow' of 1886. Despite the arctic conditions in Northumberland the fireman has managed to find a rabbit.*

Sundays and Christmas Day off. During one week in December 1900 he worked 75 hours 25 minutes and received £1 18s 4½d in wages. On one occasion he had three days' holiday.

A poem by Robert Burns, entitled 'Man Was Made to Mourn', is copied out into one of the books. Although one of its closing lines runs: 'O Death the poor man's dearest friend . . .', Miles appears to have had some fun in his hard-working life. Several pages are devoted to the organization of a village fête with tug-of-war, one-mile race, comic race, 'old men's race' and separate races for married and single ladies. There was a boys' 'high leap' and 'long leap' and a girls' skipping competition for which the prize was a 'gold broach'.

One winter Miles recorded a shift of 23 hours spent out with the snowplough. Stations, especially on branch lines, frequently became snowed up and trains were often buried in snow-drifts. A particularly bad winter was the one of 1885–6. Sir William Acworth records how a team of 50 men with three engines behind a snow-plough tried to clear the main line in Northumber-

land by forcing their way through a drift 1½ miles long and nearly 5 metres high. The officer in charge said:

We left Gateshead soon after midnight on Sunday .... If it had been daylight, we should never have attempted it. But then we came to a cutting, where the snow, falling from the banks above, had solidified the snow beneath into a compact mass; and there we stuck. From Monday morning till Saturday night none of us ever had our clothes off. For thirty-eight hours we were without water, except the melted snow, and without food. At last we got the road clear to Alnwick, and sent an engine down. The man swept the town bare, I believe; anyway, he came back with several hams, and roasts of beef, and shoulders of mutton, two or three clothes-baskets full of bread, and lots of tobacco . . .

(*The Railways of England*)

Trade unions

The first organizations run by the railway workers for themselves were benefit societies. Any combined action to improve working conditions was crushed by the railway companies; men who went on strike were sacked. Petitions asking for wage increases or other concessions were presented to the directors as 'round robins' with the signatures in a circle so that the ring-leaders could not be marked out as agitators and penalized.

Under the Reform Act of 1867 many railway-men, along with other industrial workers, gained the right to vote. Four years later, in 1871, the Amalgamated Society of Railway Servants was formed with the help of the MP for Derby, Michael Thomas Bass, who was a wealthy brewer and a director of the Midland Railway but also a supporter of humanitarian causes.

The objects of the new union were ' . . . the improvement of the general condition of all classes of railway employees; temporary assistance when thrown out of employment; legal assistance when necessary; and to provide a superannuation allowance to old and disabled members . . . .' Within a year it had 17,000

members each paying 3d a week, and its own weekly newspaper, the *Railway Service Gazette*, which later became the *Railway Review* and is now the *Transport Review*. In 1875 the ASRS opened a Railway Orphanage in Derby, which it maintained through voluntary subscriptions and flag days. Four years later it was agreed that all members should pay an extra halfpenny a week to an orphan fund.

The ASRS which amalgamated with two smaller unions in 1913 to become the National Union of Railwaymen, was a union for all grades of railway workers. Enginemen considered that their job was special and in 1880 they met at Leeds to form a craft union for drivers and firemen only – the Associated Society of Locomotive Engineers and Firemen (ASLEF), which still continues under that name today.

---

19 *On marches and demonstrations the vivid colours of the banners of different union branches made a splendid show. Many of the older ones are now preserved in the National Museum of Labour History. This is an early ASLEF one.*

LOCOMOTIVE ENGINEERS AND FIREMEN

In 1897 clerical workers formed the Railway Clerks' Association which in 1951 changed its name to the Transport Salaried Staff's Association (TSSA).

The Taff Vale case

By the end of the nineteenth century various rights had been won by trade unions. Peaceful picketing was allowed and strikers could no longer be imprisoned for 'breach of employment'. Many people thought the laws also meant that unions could not be sued for damages because of strike action by individual members. This, as a famous legal case showed, was not so.

In 1900 Taff Vale Railway Co. workers struck for higher wages, and battles went on between them and 'blackleg' labour brought in by the company's general manager. Afterwards the railway company decided to claim damages against the ASRS for losses during the strike. After a long legal wrangle the Appeal Judges in the House of Lords ruled in 1901 that the union must pay the railway company £23,000 in damages and a further £19,000 in legal costs.

This was a severe blow not only to the ASRS but to the trade union movement as a whole. Railway companies had been slow to recognize unions as negotiating bodies for their workers and the Taff Vale case was seen by the unions as evidence that employers meant to curb their growing power. Believing that working-class conditions would have to be improved by political and parliamentary methods as well as by industrial action, the ASRS was one of the first unions to become affiliated to the newly formed Labour Representation Committee which was the forerunner of the Labour Party.

1911 Strike

The first national railway strike, in which all railway unions combined to press for higher wages and improved conditions, took place in 1911. Though it lasted only two days it was a time of violence and bitterness. Troops were called

20 *The Taff Vale cheque.*

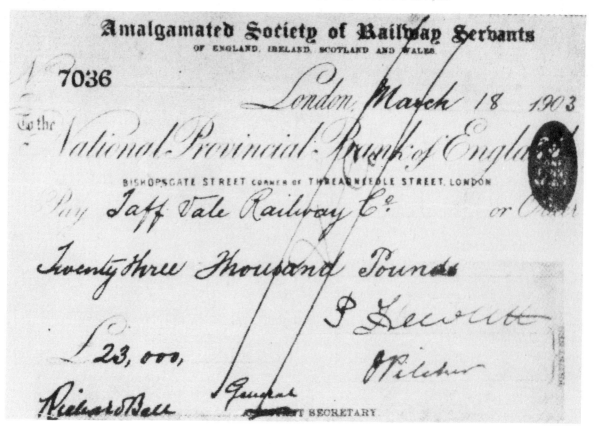

out to quell the strikers who, with the help of other trade unionists, such as the miners, had managed to bring industry to a standstill. At Llanelly in North Wales two railwaymen were killed when soldiers opened fire.

The strike led to an improvement of the conciliation boards which had been set up four years earlier for the negotiation of wages between the railway companies and their workers. Even today, wage earners on the railways are still referred to as the 'conciliation grades'.

21 *Soldiers guard Clapham Junction North signalbox during the 1911 strike.*

4 The First World War and the Depression

Industrial disputes were laid aside when the First World War broke out in 1914. With, by now, 22,000 miles of track, the railways were still Britain's major form of transport. In wartime they became vital for the movement of troops and materials, and many of their large engineering workshops were turned over to making munitions.

There were still 120 different companies ranging from the mighty Midland Railway, with 2000 miles of line and about 3000 locomotives, to the tiny Bishop's Castle Railway in Shropshire which ran for just nine miles and was the proud possessor of two engines. For wartime purposes they were all brought under Government control and run as one unit by a Railway Executive Committee.

Many railwaymen joined the forces as ordinary soldiers and others were employed in special railway units in France and Belgium. Jim Hill joined the Great Eastern Railway in 1913 as an engine cleaner and in 1915 volunteered for the Railway Operating Division of the Royal Engineers. He was sent to Poperinge in Belgium and became a fireman on ambulance trains:

... we carried a board with a large red cross on both sides of the smokebox, and to give 'Jerry' [the Germans] his due, we were never fired upon while working these trains.
(*Buckjumpers, Gobblers and Clauds*)

Those who stayed in Britain had to work doubly hard in difficult conditions. Percy Cox passed as fireman with the London and South Western Railway just before the war and was firing on the main line throughout.

We often had to work 'specials', to and from Southampton mostly – a mixed lot of trains: troop trains taking our boys to France and elsewhere; hospital trains, which we always worked very gently so as not to jolt the wounded men; and munition [ammunition] trains, which we again tried to work as smoothly as possible for our own sakes!
(*Men of the Footplate*)

Railway women

For the first time women were brought in to work on the railways in large numbers. Apart from those in the catering service, there were only about 4000 railwaywomen before 1914, most of whom were employed as cleaners or in the clerical grades. Now over 50,000 were taken on, mainly as carriage and engine cleaners, but some as ticket collectors and porters and for work in signalboxes. They were admitted to membership of the NUR in 1916. Though they had cheerfully stepped into the breach in wartime most women gave up their jobs when the men came back in 1918.

Gretna disaster

Despite the heavy casualties at the Front, a railway crash in Scotland in 1915 contributed its

---

22 *Women engine cleaners on the Lancashire & Yorkshire Railway during the First World War. Trousers were unusual for women in those days and their style of dress caused much comment.*

own blend of horror to the wartime scene. In a collision at Quintinshill, near Gretna Green, 227 people were killed, most of them men of the 7th Royal Scots Regiment travelling to Liverpool on a troop train. The accident is still on record as the worst disaster on a British railway.

1919 strike

After the war ASLEF negotiated a national standard wage system for its members which included bonuses given during the war to offset the high cost of living. The new rates meant drivers earned from 12s to 15s a day, firemen from 9s 6d to 11s and engine cleaners from 4s to 7s. They also won the right to an eight-hour day.

The NUR wanted a similar agreement, but though the Government, which still controlled the railways, agreed to pay standardized rates it would not include the bonuses.

In 1919 the NUR's members, led by their General Secretary, the Labour MP J.H. Thomas, came out on strike. To the surprise of the Government, they were joined by ASLEF which, though it had achieved its own settlement, decided to support its fellow railway union. The result was an almost complete shutdown on the railways with troops called out to guard stations, bridges and signalboxes. Fleets of lorries were organized to transport essential goods.

In a history of ASLEF published in 1921, J.R. Raynes wrote:

The strike turned all England into a nine days' wonder. While the unions remained solid to a man, and the railway stations were closed and guarded, the roads witnessed a return to something like stage coach conditions, but with motors instead of horses .... Theatrical companies moved by chars-a-banc [motor coaches], or didn't move at all; newspapers organised motor delivery, and music hall artistes packed their trappings into all sorts of vehicles. There were motor expresses for fish and other food traffic, and for nine days there was much traffic and chaos on the roads. It was the most wonderful and certainly the most spectacular

strike in history, and certainly it was most
successful.
(*Engines and Men*)

Lloyd George, the Prime Minister, who had
begun by calling the strike an 'anarchist
conspiracy' eventually agreed to negotiate and
the dispute was settled with an agreement to
standardize wage scales, starting from a basic
minimum of 51s a week. Future problems were to
be dealt with by a Central Wages Board made up
of equal numbers of union and management
representatives. In 1921 the scheme was
extended to include a consultation 'pyramid'
comprising a railway council for each line, five
sectional councils and local departmental
committees (known as LDCs) at all the larger
stations.

The 'Big Four'

The wartime experience of railway organization
led to proposals for Government control in
peacetime, but eventually it was decided to have
not one railway system, but four. Under the
Railways Act of 1921 all the different railway
companies were amalgamated to form four large
groups which had the monopoly of railway traffic
in their own areas. The 'grouping' as it was called,
came into effect on 1 January 1923.

Some of the companies now joined together
had been bitter rivals. Percy Cox recalls:

The old South-Western ceased to exist and
became part of the Southern. We did not like the
idea very much, as we thought that the other
railways, especially the South Eastern and
Chatham, would be something of a liability to our
group – you can see we had not much opinion of
those eastern lines, nor yet of the Brighton.
(*Men of the Footplate*)

As well as the Southern Railway (SR), the 'Big
Four' comprised the London, Midland & Scottish
Railway (LMS); the London & North Eastern
Railway (LNER); and the Great Western Railway
(GWR).

---

23 *An LNER train crosses Belah viaduct in County
Durham. The engine at the back is known as a 'banker';
if two engines haul the carriages from the front the train
is referred to as being 'double-headed'.*

Though it took over a few smaller lines, the GWR remained virtually unchanged and was the only one to retain its old title. Nicknamed 'God's Wonderful Railway', it was regarded with affection by staff and passengers alike. It had a particularly good safety record and in 1906 had been the first company to introduce an automatic warning device to alert a driver in the locomotive cab if he passed a signal at 'danger'.

In 1915, P.H.C. Tarr, then aged 16, joined the GWR as a greaser in the cars and waggons department at Penzance. For the next 49 years he was engaged on the meticulous behind-the-scenes work of checking, oiling, adjusting and repairing which contributed to safety on the line. 'It is surprising the number of defects which are discovered', said Mr Tarr. He became an examiner in 1924 and claimed: 'In my time I have prevented dozens of serious accidents.' He particularly remembered one day when 'I really did strike lucky'.

I was on the early shift – 6 a.m. to 2 p.m. – and my first train to examine was the 11 a.m. ex-Penzance to Paddington which had been the 1.30 p.m. Paddington to Penzance the previous day. It was a very bright morning, the sun was just rising above St Michael's Mount. The second coach was a ten-compartment, second-class coach. Stooping as always, checking everything, I noticed what appeared to be a piece of black cotton round the leading bogie's leading wheel axle. I crawled under and found it was not cotton but a split in the paint which covered the axle. With hammer and chisel I chipped and chipped until I could see a fracture in the steel axle approximately an eighth of an inch in depth and three-quarters of an inch around. Without a doubt, in a very short time it would have resulted in a very serious accident. A new bogie was ordered from Swindon and fitted at Penzance – not even safe to run to the Truro workshop.

Depression

Industrial depression was starting to bite in the 1920s with factories closing down and unemployment increasing. The railway grouping led to redundancy for many railwaymen. Others had to move to other parts of the country for jobs, which were given on the basis of 'seniority'. This meant that the man who had joined the service first was first in line for a job. It was a principle which had always been applied on the railways but now men made redundant in one area were sent to displace less senior men from another area, driving them down the ladder to take the jobs of men below them. Bob Vass had experience of these conditions after he joined the LNER as a 16-year-old engine cleaner in 1923.

I started at Heaton shed in August and in the second week in December I was paid off – finished. In the New Year I got a job at Hull Springhead shed but came back to Gateshead in March. I was sent to Tweedmouth and then transferred to Alston in Cumberland. My wages were £2 a week and we got no lodging money and no allowances. I was married by then but I had to go because if you chucked a job you were finished. I couldn't afford lodgings so I slept in the messroom on a bag of straw – what we call a 'donkey's breakfast'. The booking clerk had a farm and he used to give me a few cracked eggs for my breakfast. The messroom was full of mice and black beetles, so I couldn't keep food on the table, I had to hang it up from the ceiling.

In 1930 I was paid off again, then they finished with the boy porters and put us in their place. I was transferred to Ashington as a porter. It wasn't bad but it wasn't much of a job really. Next they made me a telegraph messenger – a man doing a boy's job. Then they put me in a signal cabin as a book lad and after that I went on a telegraph gang putting up telegraph poles. Later on I became a labourer at Ferryhill shed but it took the war to make me a fireman. I became a driver in 1947.

Wilson Cornforth, a sidings checker, became secretary of the Darlington No. 1 branch of the NUR in 1922 and for him the Depression meant a lot of work dealing with the extra problems of branch members. It also caused changes in his household. His daughter recalls that it

not only filled our small house with all the

equipment attached to that office but with a greatly increased number of callers. Members came to pay their dues or discuss claims for compensation, or draw sickness benefit . . . . In the confined space of the living room the management of both domestic and trade union administration caused a few problems . . . . The opening and closing of the front door did no good to the bread set to rise in a large brown bowl on the hearth. Bathing was another tricky business. A galvanised bath . . . was brought in front of the fire on Friday nights. I could enjoy the warm soapy comfort of it until there was a knock at the door whereupon I was bundled into a towel and sent into the scullery . . . . Struggling widows, disabled men, distraught workers threatened with redundancy, came to our house to explain the causes of their distress, get their documents witnessed, their claims presented. Father's role was confessor, advocate, paymaster . . . . I knew about letters of administration, percentage disability, the promotion ladder and seniority of service almost before I could tie my own shoelaces . . . .

(Lena Wilson, *The Sunshine Casts No Shadows*)

General Strike

Similar conditions prevailed in other industries and in May 1926 the miners, faced with big pay cuts, went on strike. The railway unions joined others in support when asked by the TUC to back a General Strike.

In Darlington Wilson Cornforth became secretary of the joint strike committee with its headquarters at the Temperance Institute. It paid out strike benefit to members, directed pickets, issued permits for the movement of essential supplies, supervised despatch riders and produced daily bulletins of strike news.

The Secretary, and other members took in camp beds so that they could remain on duty or on call day and night. Wives and daughters carried food to them each day. Many committee men finally emerged with a ten days' growth of beard.

(*The Long Hard Road*)

Round-the-clock 'rota committees' were formed and kept a log-book of events. Written in pencil in a black school exercise book, it brings back vividly the excitement and dedication of those days:

Telegram received from Head Office stating: Position solid as a rock . . . . Request for permit to convey little girl to Witton . . . resolved that picket secretary endeavour to secure a motor car . . . . Men detailed to feed and care for horses at Bank Top . . . . Request . . . to remove bananas from Bank Top – refused . . . . Report – two men blacklegging at Croft Junction . . . . Disturbance . . . in Priestgate where police made a baton charge . . . . Reports from Durham all standing firm . . . . All buses off the streets in Newcastle

24 *A poster issued by the NUR against further wage cuts in 1932.*

.... **Two destroyers and a Submarine arrived in the Tyne.... Despatch rider from Sunderland... has no means of procuring petrol. Half a gallon supplied ....**

The strike ended in bitterness and disappointment for the unions. The continuing Depression meant that not only the miners but many other workers including the railwaymen had to agree to wage reductions in the 1930s.

The railway companies were losing money. Competition from road haulage firms, the buses and private cars meant that the 'iron road' was no longer supreme in the transport world. By 1935 nearly half the railway's goods traffic and many of its passengers had deserted to the motor vehicle.

Speed records

Nevertheless, trains continued to fire the imaginations of many. Crack expresses like the LMS *Royal Scot* sped over the rails in speed attempts reminiscent of the 'Race to the North' in the 1890s, when the east and west coast lines had vied to achieve a record time to Scotland.

In 1928 the LNER's famous Pacific class engine No. 4472, *Flying Scotsman*, became the first to do a regular non-stop run from London to Edinburgh. The journey took eight and a half hours and as it was impossible for a driver and fireman to work continuously for so long on such a powerful engine, Nigel Gresley, the LNER's locomotive engineer, designed a corridor-tender to connect the driving cab with the first coach of the train. Halfway to Scotland a spare crew walked through to take over.

In 1935 Gresley introduced the first streamlined locomotive, Pacific A4 class No. 2509, *Silver Link*, which reached 112 m.p.h. on the run north. Three years later his newest A4, No. 4468, *Mallard*, broke the world speed record for steam, which it still holds, with a time of 126 m.p.h.

Restaurant cars

The development of bigger and faster engines was matched by an increase in passenger comforts, including catering. The first-ever restaurant car had run on the Great Northern Railway in 1879. It was owned by the American

25 *The* Flying Scotsman *locomotive on the turntable at Grantham, Lincs, in 1931. Confusion sometimes arises because the express train service between King's Cross and Edinburgh was also named the "Flying Scotsman". It was often hauled by the* Flying Scotsman *locomotive but other engines also did the job.*

Pullman Company and had a kitchen at one end with a coal-fired range. In 1891 the GER had introduced a corridor train with its own dining cars for all passengers.

Between the wars railway dining facilities were still a mixture of Pullman and company-run cars. An all-Pullman train service, the *Brighton Belle*, was started by the SR in 1933 and people had to pay extra to travel on it. Even to third-class ticket holders, however, ordinary restaurant cars usually served a four-course lunch or dinner and offered a comprehensive wine-list.

As a boy of 15, Harry Gosling started with the Pullman Co. in 1936.

They kept us on the go. It was all silver then and it all had to be cleaned. We did the knives in a machine with the old brown powder. At first we did that and the washing up but after about a month we were allowed in the car to see if we could get our 'sea legs'. On the trains you had to be dedicated but I was determined that I wanted to learn the job. I did training in cocktails in the American Bar at Charing Cross Hotel and my first job was as a junior attendant serving drinks and sandwiches on the Metropolitan Line. I got £3 5s

27 *The Cornish Riviera express – on its way to West Country holiday resorts – travels under a signal gantry at Reading. The fish-tailed signals are the 'distant' ones. If a 'distant' is at caution the driver must slow down until he sees the 'home' signal which is near to the box which controls it. If this is up – or 'on' as railwaymen call it – he must stop. In this picture the signals for the Cornish Riviera are 'off', which means the 'road' is clear. Most semaphore signal gantries like this have now been replaced by colour-light signals, which resemble road traffic-lights but are more complex.*

a month and 5s was stopped for uniform. Pullman was a non-union firm at that time and they didn't pay overtime, but we got tips. In the old days people with money always travelled Pullman.

Harry did 50 years as a restaurant-car steward, or 'attendant' as it was then called, and says: 'If I had my life over again I would do just the same.' He even named his son Adrian after one of the cars on the *Thanet Belle*.

David Lovering became an attendant on the restaurant-car service between Exeter and Waterloo in 1939.

26 *David Lovering, fourth from left, poses for a picture with fellow members of the restaurant car service.*

Our wages were 12s 6d a week. We relied on tips and if anyone gave us 6d or 1s we thought we were well in. We did a twelve-hour day and at

first when you got off on to the platform you were swaying. After three or four days you got acclimatized. You had to learn balance.

Excursions

Between the wars the railway companies competed to persuade people to travel by rail to holiday resorts in their areas. Guards' and ticket collectors' jobs were complicated by a host of tickets for different categories of traveller. There were special rates for anglers, entertainers, fishworkers, transmigrants and shipwrecked mariners. 'Ships' crews and parties of whalers', 'friends and relatives of ocean passengers', and 'commercial travellers, weekend' were among those who got reduced fares. There was an extensive code of 'ticket nips' to indicate where a ticket was clipped.

28 Ticket 'nips' for Scottish stations, including Tay Bridge, illustrated in a booklet of 'Instructions to Station Masters and other Staff engaged in the Examination and Collection of Tickets', dated 1927.

North Leith.	
St. Fort, Bogside.	
Leven, Bonnybridge, Oakley (Fife). Campsie Glen, Polton.	
Dysart, Forest Mill.	
Eskbank, Causewayhead.	
Methil, Balado, Clackmannan and Kennet, Kilpatrick.	
Roxburgh, Inverkeithing.	
Kippen, Markinch.	
Dundee (Tay Bridge), Bowling.	
Burntisland, Bo'ness, Westerton.	
Newport (East), Causewayend, Croy.	
Crook of Devon, Bonnybridge (Central), Morar, Thornton (for break of journey and re-booking).	
Knowesgate.	
Newport (West), Eyemouth, Dalmuir.	
Eskbridge, Tillicoultry, Dunfermline (Upper) (for Workmen's Trains).	
Burnmouth, Cowdenbeath (for Workmen's Trains).	
Sauchie, Twechar.	
Haymarket (for cancelling collected tickets only).	
Musselburgh, Broomieknowe Aberfoyle, Whitburn, Selkirk, Charlestown.	
Kilsyth, Dolphinton, Singer.	
Lower Bathgate, Torrance Dollar, Auchendinny.	
Hawthornden, Tayport, Stirling (E. and G.).	
Lennoxtown, Rosyth (Halt).	
Craigendoran, Rothbury, Forth Ferry Boat.	
Cowlairs (for cancelling collected tickets only), Rawyards, Bonnyrigg, Roslin.	
North Berwick, Pomathorn, Kincardine, Mallaig, Mount Melville, Easter Road.	
Commonhead, Bervie, Rosslynlee, Gairlochy, Dullatur.	
Millerhill, Dundee (Esplanade), Crossgatehall (Halt).	

5 From the Second World War to Nationalization

On the outbreak of war in 1939 the railways were immediately faced with the immense task of evacuating civilians from London and other big cities. During three days in September, nearly 4,000 special trains took over a million evacuees, most of them children, to safer places in country areas.

Once again the railways were a key part of the war effort. So, though many railwaymen joined the armed forces, many others were directed to remain in their jobs. They were joined by thousands of women recruits.

The wartime 'blackout' meant that every colour-light signal had to be hooded, the windows of singalboxes bricked up, and locomotive cabs covered to hide the glow from the firebox. Stations and marshalling yards operated under dim lights which had to be put out altogether during air raids. As well as their ordinary duties, staff had to take on firewatching shifts. During the Blitz Stan Joby was a fireman at Stratford, East London. His son, R.S. Joby, recalls what it was like:

...the whole East End suddenly had to cope with pandemonium .... The carriage sidings just up the line were hit and carriages set alight .... Incendiary bombs had to be smothered by shunters and footplate crew the moment they flared. Old sacks, buckets of sand, stirrup pumps, tarpaulins, anything to hand was used .... While the civilian population sought shelter ... the railwaymen carried on under fire.
(*The Railwaymen*)

Posters asking 'Is Your Journey Really

29 *The destruction of Coventry station during the blitz.*

Necessary?' were put up to discourage people from travelling. Carriage windows were painted black and the coaches lit at night by eerie blue lamps. Stations had their name-boards painted over in case of German invasion and white lines were put along the platform edges to stop people falling on the track in the dark.

Railways, of course, were prime targets for enemy bombers. In *Men of the Footplate* Albert Young relates:

I was driving a train north the night Coventry was blitzed. We were warned at Rugby there would be danger .... Then, just before Nuneaton, I saw one of the raiders actually flying low and following my train. There was a bridge not far ahead ... I told my fireman to work hard and get as much coal on the fire as he could. I then told him to close the firehole door and leave the dampers open. As a result we made more smoke than I ever remember seeing come from any engine before. It certainly covered us and our train pretty effectively .... Soon after, down came the bombs, but they were very badly aimed and did no damage ... we got over the bridge and finished our run safely.

Nationalization

There was no return to the 'Big Four' after the war. The Labour Government elected in 1945 had

36

nationalization of the railways high on its list of priorities. The Railway Executive Committee which had run the railways during the war continued to operate them until 'vesting day' on 1 January 1948, when they came under public ownership. Now called British Railways, they were divided into six regions and had as their new symbol a lion standing over a wheel.

Railwaymen celebrated the achievement of a goal which had first been advocated by the ASRS in 1894, but in practice nationalization made little difference to their everyday lives. Derek Cornforth started work as a signalbox boy during the war and was made secretary of Darlington No. 1 branch on the retirement of his father,

---

30 *Title page of the new British Railways' Rule Book, which replaced those of the individual 'Big Four' companies.*

31 *Derek Cornforth with the banner made for the centenary of the NUR's Darlington No. 1 branch in 1972.*

Wilson Cornforth, in 1967. He remembers: 'We didn't feel it was a question of the workers taking over but we did feel the industry would be revitalized. I think that people did feel that with the different companies going out, it would all be one.'

Catering

In the austere conditions of post-war Britain coal was in short supply and clothes and food were still rationed. This made railway catering difficult. Bob Dalley became a Pullman car chef in 1946 after wartime service in the Royal Army Catering Corps. He served 15 years on the *Bournemouth Belle* and also worked on the *Golden Arrow* and the *Tees–Tyne Pullman*. On his first day he cooked 88 lunches.

I had to do the ordering from the Pullman stores every day and supplies were taken down to the train by hamper. In those days you took anything you could get – potatoes, apples, perhaps a big fish, semolina, powdered soup. There was no

sugar and the passengers went wild if they saw a bit of white bread. You had to make up your own menus from what you'd got and each car had to try and get the profit percentage up. We were allocated one bottle of whisky and one bottle of sherry a week – we almost charged for a glass of water.

Peter Murrin, now a chief steward, started as a GWR page boy at Paddington in 1946 and did everything from scrubbing floors to cleaning the Chief Steward's shoes. He remembers:

There were no buffet cars then, only restaurant cars, and we used to keep filling them up with different sittings until we ran out of food. Food was rationed but the chefs could do wonders with whale meat and goat. They had a mincer and that never stopped. Whale smelt of fish and they had to try and erode it with onions and spices. They used to call it 'Sauté of meat' – there was no Trade Descriptions Act in those days.

The Pullman Company was taken over by BR in 1954 and the hours and wages of the staff gradually came into line with those of other railway workers. Bob Dalley:

Before we were taken over there was no such thing as hours, days or even weeks. We didn't have a day off for a month sometimes. If you asked for one they'd say: 'You had one five weeks ago . . .' We got to know our regulars and the more you looked after them the more you made out of the day. That was what it was all about. You had to do it because you didn't get the wages.

P-way work

In 1955 when Harry Lofkin started on the permanent way much of the work was done in the same way as it had been since the nineteenth century. He found that as a lengthman in a small maintenance gang looking after a mile of the four-line track near Crewe:

It was almost like a family, really. I didn't like working indoors and for me the P-way is a marvellous life. There is a great spirit amongst P-way men though a lot of people outside, including other railwaymen, look down on them. Each stretch used to have a cabin and most of the old ones had coal fires. There was always someone who arrived to get the fire going first thing. Old lengthmen used to know everything about their stretch of track, all the history of it – when the wires were changed, when new drains were put in – for years back.

Every maintenance man worked weekends. It just became a habit over the years. It sometimes caused a lot of trouble at home but it was the money you couldn't do without. I would often complete a day and finish at 5 o'clock and arrive home to find the caller-out there – we didn't have telephones then – and I had to return immediately. If you did that you went on overtime. Fog and snow duties were extra. With snow everything was by shovel. I have been kept on at the end of a day and told to stay on snow duties until midnight, clearing points and so on. Until the tracks were clear you didn't get a break. Youngsters today would say: 'I'm going for my break' – and good luck to them. If we'd done that we would have been sent home and I had three children so I couldn't afford to lose the money. With fog we had to put detonators on the track to warn the driver he was approaching a signal. Every time a train went over it you had to put another detonator down. On a cold night – by midnight you really were cold!

Soon permanent-way work began to change. New machines for everything from aligning the rails and packing ballast to hedge cutting and weed spraying brought new problems. As an NUR officer and chairman of the Crewe LDC, Harry had to deal with many welfare problems, among them helping members claim compensation for deafness.

Lots and lots of P-way men became deaf because of the machines. Long pieces of steel were punched home with a tremendous banging, tamping machines lifted the tracks and punched the stones in each side, drills were really loud. In the early days there were no such things as ear

32 *A track re-laying gang in the 1950s. Compare this with the modern methods used by similar gangs in the 1980s, as shown in the frontispiece picture.*

muffs and it was always just expected that men would become deaf on the P-way.

The familiar sound of trains going clickety-clack over the 'metals' ended on main lines in the 1960s with the advent of the welded rail. This replaced the old 60 ft lengths with continuous sections of track extending for well over 1,000 ft and laid on concrete sleepers. Length gangs no longer needed to spend their time tightening and oiling bolts and attending to the wooden sleepers. Though for BR mechanization meant a big reduction in maintenance costs, for the lengthman it meant the end of his P-way 'family'.

Harry, now a timekeeper at Crewe, says:

Today P-way work is a totally different job. There are big mobile gangs instead of the small gangs we had and a lot of the *esprit de corps* has gone. Machine operators tend to grow apart from the men on the track. They travel long distances and the groups are broken up.

Engine sheds

For the first ten years after the war steam was still the major form of locomotive power. Drivers from that era still reminisce about the days when engine sheds were 'like something out of Dickens'. Jackie Moore started as an engine cleaner at Gateshead shed in 1940.

---

33 *Locomotives lined up at Darlington round shed.*

The place was one mass of stinking yellow smoke. You could just see the engines peering out of the smog. They were in bays of eight – Pacifics – and the soot lay on the top of them like velvet. In three hours they were spotless.

Top drivers had their 'own' engines and fussed over them like mother hens, bringing their own oil from home and touching up the paintwork themselves. Running sheds were close communities with their own customs and jargon. Most drivers were never called by their real names at all. A new engine cleaner would be flummoxed when asked to find 'Captain Blast', 'Cat's Milk' or 'Tea-party Dan'.

Lodging turns

Steam engines, using a ton of coal for roughly every 60 miles, were becoming increasingly heavy and powerful, and journey times were getting shorter. Trainmen still had to do 'lodging

34 *Len Fairbairn (left) as a young fireman in 1946, with driver Frankie McCardle.*

turns', however, on long runs. This meant staying the night in lodging houses or railway hostels before returning to home-base. On freight trains men were sometimes away for three or four days at a time. In 'digs' before the war 'often you would have to queue to get into bed. It was by no means uncommon to have to share a double bed with a man you had never seen before, and the sheets were never very often changed . . .' (C.H. Simmons in *Men of the Footplate*.)

Newcastle driver Len Fairbairn remembers the post-war railway lodging house at Kentish Town as still very primitive. 'There were dormitories with white brick walls. The beds were in cubicles and if someone snored it went right along the line.'

ASLEF strike

In the 1950s the railways, still recovering from the battering they had taken during the war, began to lose passengers and freight traffic to road transport even faster than they had done in the 1930s.

Despite public ownership, BR was still expected to be run as a commercial enterprise rather than, as many railwaymen and others had hoped, a public service. Railwaymen's wages had to be balanced against railway profits. In 1955 many industrial workers were getting wage increases but the basic pay of railwaymen, at a little over £7 a week, was £2 below that of most of them.

Footplatemen had always earned more than other railway workers, but now their differentials (the gap between their wages and those of other grades) were narrowing. So in 1955 ASLEF members went on strike. The NUR did not support them and drivers who were members of the all-grades union continued to work while their colleagues were 'out'. This caused hostility between the two unions and in some cases between father and son, or between two brothers who belonged to different unions.

Afterwards, the Guillebaud Report on railway pay recommended that fair and reasonable wages should be given to railway workers in line with the amounts received by workers in comparable industries such as gas and electricity, engineering and the Health Service. Enginemen got a small increase.

Modernization

British Railways decided on a large-scale modernization scheme which meant not only improved track, more power signalboxes and faster freight waggons, but also the end of steam. After 130 years of service, from *Locomotion* to *Mallard*, the steam engine was to be made redundant. The last one to be built was completed at Swindon Works in 1960. It was named *Evening Star*.

By this time nearly 5000 steam engines had been thrown on the scrapheap – in most cases literally, though a good few were rescued by preservation societies and museums. They were replaced by diesel-powered locomotives and, for shorter journeys, diesel multiple-unit vehicles, known as DMUs. There were also electric

vehicles, especially on the Southern Region where electrification by means of a third rail had already taken place.

Driver Stanley Watson became an engine cleaner at Woodford Halse in 1944. Then, as a 'passed cleaner', he graduated to firing on yard shunters.

It was all steam trains then but in 1958, coming over Birdcage Bridge outside Rugby I saw a 2,000 h.p. diesel leaving the platform. It was the first diesel I had ever seen in reality and it intrigued me. I couldn't get it out of my mind. A beautiful green thing it was. I said to my wife: 'I want to go

35 *An LMS saddle-tank engine ends its days at Derby scrapyard.*

to Rugby. That is where things are going to happen.' I applied for a firing position there and got it.

After a few years as a driver he learnt diesel traction and since the electrification of the west coast main line has driven electric locomotives. He retains a soft spot for steam.

I was glad I was part of it. Steam – it was the nearest thing we ever got to building a living robot. One day she – we always called steam engines 'she' – would behave perfectly; the next day she could act all temperamental. We don't call electric locos anything. They don't appear to have any heart to them.

In Newcastle, driver Tommy Smith agreed.

Diesels are just boxes on wheels. They are wonderful machines but they have no character. Steam engines were all different, like people. Take the *Flying Scotsman*, for instance. I've fired her and driven her. She may have been a canny engine when she was breaking records but in my day she was a really bad engine. With her you had to put more on the shovel than most engines and really pull the stops out to keep her going. She was sluggish. On some engines you could shut the steam off and she would still run. On the 4472 you could never do that. You might use two tons more coal from Edinburgh to London on her than on a good engine. I have seen strong firemen grow white when given the *Flying Scotsman*, and the *Mallard* was not so good either.

Tommy went in the Navy in 1943 but he always intended to be an engine driver like his father and started as an engine cleaner at Heaton shed while still on demob leave in 1947. Starting with a box Brownie camera which he bought when he joined the railways, he has, over 40 years, built up a unique collection of railway photographs. 'I feel sorry for the youngsters today' he says. 'We had steam engines with character and so many branch lines it was like the spokes of a wheel. Now there are diesels and far fewer lines to work.'

36 *Fireman Tommy Smith is dwarfed by the* Owain Glyndwr *at Kingmoor shed, Carlisle, in the late 1950s. The shape of things to come is indicated by the 'flash' on the side of the steam engine warning footplatemen about electrification of the line.*

6 The Changing Railway

The branch lines received their death sentence in 1963 with the Beeching Report. Dr Richard Beeching, the new chairman of the British Railways Board, proposed, in a document entitled 'The Reshaping of British Railways', to cut services which were losing money. The 'Beeching Axe', as it was soon called, meant the withdrawal of passenger trains from 5000 of BR's 17,830 miles of line, the closure of over 2000 of its 7000 stations, a drastic reduction in the number of coal depots and goods yards, and the replacement of most of the small 'pick-up' goods trains by non-stop, long-distance freight trains. For many railway workshops it meant a substantial reduction in the workforce; for others, complete closure.

Redundancies affected all railway staff. More than 500,000 people had been employed on BR in 1960 but by 1970 the numbers had dropped to 273,000. Staff numbers and track miles had reverted to the position on Victorian railways a hundred years earlier.

Changes

In 1964 British Railways changed its name to British Rail and adopted a symbol of double arrows. The Penzance Agreement, so called because negotiations took place while the NUR's annual meeting was held there in 1966, brought more changes and new rates of pay based on a minimum £13 for a 40-hour week, though all grades earned more through overtime and Sunday working. In 1968 British Rail Engineering Ltd (BREL) was set up as a separate body to run the bigger railway workshops, including those at Derby, Crewe and Swindon.

Porters

Old job titles and old styles of uniform disappeared. Many passengers, already angered by the closure of the small country stations and branch lines, were particularly sad to see the demise of the station porter. Amongst other duties he had carried their luggage, announced the arrival and departure of trains, stoked the waiting-room fire and tended the station flowerbeds. He had also been the butt of numerous music-hall jokes and songs, one of the most popular of which began:

> Oh, Mr Porter, what shall I do?
> I wanted to go to Birmingham,
> And they've carried me on to Crewe!

Somehow the new categories of junior, senior and leading railman did not seem the same.

Area manager

Out, too, went the station master. Regions are now subdivided into Areas under an Area manager with, below him, various operational managers and a traffic manager who takes over most of the duties – but not the top hat – of the station master. Larger stations have station managers.

John Brazier became Area manager at Rugby in 1979 and was transferred to Coventry when the Area was extended in 1983. It now covers a 70-mile stretch of the west coast main line, has freight lines serving a colliery, a solid-fuel production plant and two oil terminals; it takes in ten staffed and two unstaffed stations, and has a total staff of over 600. Like so many on the railways, from Victorian times down to today, John Brazier comes from a railway family.

I was born in a railway house at Ferrybridge in Yorkshire, where my father was a porter. He fixed me up on the railways. I would have liked to have stopped on at school and got into science but there were five in our family so there was not much hope of that, family-wise. Having gone in I never wanted to be anywhere else.

He started at the age of 16 in 1952 as a junior clerk at Knaresborough and worked his way up through various clerical grades, through goods agent and station manager, to assistant Area manager at Derby before becoming Area manager at Rugby.

I started just after nationalization and I started on the steam railway, so that was a big change, steam to diesel. Then there was the Beeching era. It is still a changing railway now. One big difference is that there is much more contact between the Board and on-ground management. We are consulted more and there is also a lot more communication between us and the staff.

Chris Taylor, who became traffic manager at Nuneaton in 1981, agrees.

When I started in 1967 as a junior clerk it was still very regimental. The discipline system was very military. Most of the old station masters were real so-and-sos and chief clerks could be real tyrants too. Now it is much more relaxed. There has been a complete change in attitude since I joined. Unless it is a very formal occasion, my staff call me 'Chris'. There is also less supervision. More

37 *An old-style goods train at a branch-line station in Scotland.*

and more people are being allowed to do their own job. It makes blokes more self-reliant, more responsible. They know that if anything goes wrong, their head is on the chopping block. I like it because it is self-regulating. You know what you have to do and you do it. It would take a very large crowbar to shift me off the railway.

New developments

When the diesels were introduced the job of fireman vanished and with it the skills of the

steam-locomotive running shed. The traditional line of promotion no longer applied, so locomotive grades were reclassified as traction trainee, driver's assistant and driver.

BR introduced single-manning for shorter diesel and electric locomotive journeys. Drivers disliked it: they felt a second person was still needed in the cab. Colin Forster, who started at Gateshead shed in 1946 and worked as both fireman and driver on steam, says: 'Single-manning has made the job lonely. Men used to work with the same people they had worked with for maybe 40 years. Now it's lonely and you find your mind can wander.'

On the freight side, new developments included merry-go-round trains which travelled between pit and power-station unloading coal on a conveyor system; and freightliners carrying

---

38 *Traffic manager Chris Taylor visits one of the signalboxes in his area.*

sealed containers for transfer to road vehicles at special terminals. Stan Watson feels railways have the edge in competition with road transport. 'I can drive the equivalent of 30 vehicle-loads from here to Manchester in 1 hour 35 minutes.'

In 1975 BR signed a closed-shop agreement with the unions and in 1981 it put to them proposals for a series of changes which it felt would lead to greater efficiency and economy. They included an extension of single-manning; the removal of guards from freight, and some pasenger, trains; and a shift system known as 'flexible rostering'.

The unions saw the proposals as a way of cutting costs by losing jobs and feared a threat to safety on the railway. After negotiations the NUR agreed that guards should work a 39-hour-week in shifts varying between seven and nine hours. ASLEF was rigidly opposed to this variation of shift times and did not want to give up the hard-won eight-hour day. In 1982 a series of strikes took place and though agreement was eventually reached, many ASLEF members, and also some NUR guards, are still bitter about the new rosters and manning arrangements.

Len Fairbairn, who is secretary of the drivers' LDC at Newcastle, says:

We used to fight to improve conditions. Now we are fighting to maintain them and in the last few years we have been losing. They are demanding more and more from us. They want us on our own nine hours a day, but if things don't go right, what do you do? I think they are going towards the safety line.

BR, however, maintains that 'safety is paramount'. It states that its policy is 'not to introduce changes which would endanger safety' and points with pride to the fact that railways are the safest form of travel. While over 6000 people are killed on Britain's roads *each year*, only 51 passengers were killed on the railways in the *ten years* between 1976 and 1985.

High Speed Trains

In 1973 new High Speed Trains which could

39   *View from the driving cab of a High Speed Train.*

travel at 141 m.p.h. were put into service and were the foreruners of the InterCity 125 trains which today run between Britain's major cities. Trains travelling at 100 m.p.h. or more still have two drivers who take turns at the controls. There are also various regulations providing for double-manning on journeys of longer than the average time or length.

HSTs are powered by diesel units at the front and rear. The cab has built-in safety devices which ensure that should the driver collapse at the controls the brakes will automatically come on. An automatic warning system alerts him if he passes a signal at 'danger'.

Driving an HST demands total concentration. With a co-driver, Colin Forster frequently does the 538-mile run from Newcastle to King's Cross and back.

They say there is more romance with steam, but it was harder physical work. Diesels are a different kettle of fish. We do three days on the Newcastle–King's Cross run then have a break. It is plenty. It is not manual work but even though you know the route and the different speeds on it, you have to be alert all the time. The job needs a lot of concentration.

colour test.' There is also an annual driving assessment by an inspector and route cards have to be signed every six months.

Stan considers the initial task of 'learning the road' the most boring job a driver faces.

They give you as long as you like to learn it and you do it a bit at a time. You have to 'sign the road' when you feel you are competent to take a train over that route. It would be your folly to 'sign a road' when you were not aware of it. You sign that you are fully competent, fully aware of every signal, every station. For example, coming to Rugby you are beginning to put the brake on one and a half miles away. We have no leeway for those words 'I think'. We have to *know*. We have no leeway for suppositions. It has to be spot-on every time.

In steam days drivers were more highly regarded by the community than they are now. Stan: 'My father was a 100 per cent locoman. He started in 1908 and when he started engine drivers were very much looked up to.'

On the links

When Stan Watson started at Rugby there were 15 links; now there are only three. They have 26 men in each. Drivers arrive 15 minutes early for a shift and after passing an inspection in which, among other points, a check is made to see that they have not been drinking, they collect a 'diagram' of their route. They then study operating notices about engineering works, line blockages, speed restrictions, signalling and permanent-way alterations. Most important is the late-notice board on which all last-minute changes and restrictions are posted.

Drivers have regular medical checks and eyesight tests. Vision must be perfect when they join but they are allowed glasses later if needed. Colour vision is very important. Tests are more sophisticated now than when Colin Forster joined. 'The chief clerk slung a ravel of wool at me and told me to pick out six colours. That was the

41 *Drivers and guards on a route-learning 'special'. The 'road' on freight lines and in goods and marshalling yards has to be learnt in the same way as main-line and other passenger routes.*

48

The respect stemmed in part from the romance of the job. To be an engine driver was said to be every boy's dream. Colin: 'At the start of railways for a man to become an engine driver must have been tantamount to becoming an astronaut today.'

Shifts

Even so, shift work has always been one of the drawbacks of the job. 'Last week,' says Stan, 'I was starting at 3 a.m. People do find it a bit of a bind getting up at 2 or 3 in the morning but on the other hand, when you finish, you have got the rest of the day to yourself.'

Dave Sursham is a spare-link driver at Newcastle, which means he has to drive any type of train as required. He says:

My wife doesn't like the shifts. You can't make

arrangements especially as, with flexible rostering, the starting time has a two-hour margin on each side and the length of the shift could be from seven to nine hours. On the spare link there are 88 different starting times. You do know which days you get off, but it does make social life rather difficult.

As a driver's assistant at Waterloo, Paul James finds that 'The shifts are killing sometimes.' He and his girlfriend, who works for a bus company, are buying a house together, but the shift system means that 'Some days I don't see her at all.'

As a traction trainee in 1986 Paul, then aged 19, did a six-week course at a BR training school. Before qualifying for the 27-week drivers' course he will have to be 21½ and have done 500 trips, or served for two and a half years, as a driver's assistant.

Vandalism and other hazards

Among the things Paul is already learning at first hand are the kind of hazards facing a modern

42 *Colin Forster (left) and Dave Sursham stand beside an HST at Newcastle Central Station.*

43 *A vandalized shunting 'pilot' loco at Jarrow yard in 1985. Says Tommy Smith, who took the picture, 'Every window and everything in the cab was smashed. Inside it was in a disgusting state and the detonators had been stolen. We used to leave the "pilots" out in the yard; now we have to put them in the shed overnight.'*

explaining about the dangers of 25,000 volt cables?'; he has been doing it ever since.

British Transport Police also visit schools, and another way they tackle vandalism is by running Q-trains. Named after the armed ships in World War Two which were disguised as merchant vessels, they look like passenger trains but carry only police and railway staff. 'Every day you go out with one you catch some', says Dave Sursham.

Dave has had his share of violence.

On my first journey after I was made a driver a log off a tree came straight through the middle window. That was my baptism. On the same route a bit later a hammer head came through the window. Luckily I wasn't hit either time. I just heard an almighty smash. Another time I saw three little 'uns – no more than 10 or 11 years old – taking up handfuls of stones to throw. I gave a good blow on the whistle and it frightened them off. Stones and stuff from bridges are the most frequent and I think it is getting worse.

Trains today travel at such high speeds that they cannot stop quickly if something – or someone – is on the line. An HST, for example, takes a mile to pull up. So when Dave, driving back from Edinburgh one Sunday morning, saw a figure on the track, there was nothing he could do.

driver. These include obstructions placed on the track, trains damaged by vandals and objects thrown at the driving-cab windows.

You have to be aware of hazards all the time. On the train the other day we were going under a bridge and something hit the window and it cracked and split. We had to stop the train and leave it. We couldn't go on like that.

Children are among the worst culprits. At Rugby, Stan is one of a number of drivers who give talks on vandalism to schools and show videos about the dangers of playing on the line. In 1960 he managed to recover 12 detonators stolen from a signalbox. Afterwards the Area manager asked him 'how about you going into schools and

We took the bend after Morpeth and were on the 100 m.p.h. stretch to Heaton. It was a straight track and a person came from behind a bridge. He stood in the middle of the track facing the engine. He had an anorak on and he put his hood up over his head. Instantaneously I blew the whistle and put the brake on. I had no chance of stopping before I hit him. I just shut my eyes and turned my head and waited for the thud. My co-driver went for assistance. For two nights afterwards I don't think I slept at all. They wanted me to take time off but I went straight back. I don't know if I was right or not.

7 Working on the Railways Today and Prospects for Tomorrow

High speed trains call for fast food. Freezers and microwaves have changed train catering almost beyond recognition since the days when Bob Dalley cooked by coal gas: 'and we didn't have a fridge we had an ice-box: two blocks of ice in a cupboard'.

Shorter journeys have meant more buffet cars, but BT still runs Pullman cars and complete Pullman trains providing more leisurely meals. Linda Burns joined BR's Travellers' Fare in 1978 and is now chief stewardess on the Yorkshire Pullman. During a 15-hour shift she does two 'up' and two 'down' trips between Leeds and London serving breakfast, lunch, tea and dinner to passengers.

We have three days on – not necessarily consecutive – and three days off. When I'm on I get a taxi to the siding to get the restaurant car ready at 5.30 a.m. On the last run we arrive back in Leeds at 8.15 p.m.

An essential of the job is to keep smiling.

One of the passengers said to me once: 'You

---

44 *Ishwar Lad (left) talks to fellow chargeman Colin Ledsham, who is driving a tractor for pulling the 'brutes' (seen behind Ishy) used for loading parcels.*

were smiling this morning at 7 o'clock and you are still smiling this evening.' Most of the regulars are great. A few are really nasty but with most you can have a right laugh.

Rugby station

Dickens's 'Mugby' station now has a Travellers' Fare buffet on the platform serving a variety of snacks to passengers. In Victorian times the town, a busy railway junction, had three stations but now only the last to be built remains. When the 'down' side was opened in 1885 a dance was held on the quarter-mile long platform and 2000 people cavorted to the music of the Steam Shed Band. Now over 200 non-stop express trains thunder through each day. On an average weekday, however, more than 100 passenger trains do stop and there are also numerous freight trains.

In an office off the platform a modern telex machine contrasts sharply with the station's Victorian stonework. Chargeman Ishwar Lad says:

It shows all train movements. It will tell me exactly which signal a train is coming through at a given time. I am responsible for despatching trains, seeing that the carriage doors are shut, helping passengers, and everything to do with newspapers, mail and parcels.

Born in Tanzania, son of a railwayman, Ishy, as he is known, came to England in 1965. His brother was already with BR. Having started as a railman at the age of 19, Ishy is now in charge of the platform under the station supervisor. He says:

When I started there was a lot more respect for station staff. Nowadays people have got no manners. They don't say 'thank-you' and they always blame the railway. If they miss a train they blame us.

He concedes:

We do get thanks sometimes. On one occasion we put up a ramp for a disabled woman and she wrote a nice letter to thank us. Another time a girl was travelling to Birmingham to sit an exam and her train had to terminate because of snow. We pulled the express in for her at Rugby – it was not a scheduled stop – and she got there in time. Afterwards she wrote to tell us she had passed the exam. That sort of thing makes for a really happy family.

Office work

In the booking office Mervyn Dearlove, who has been a booking clerk for ten years, agrees that passengers can be difficult.

Sometimes they are really nice and sometimes they are having a go at you. You don't get bored when you are dealing with the public. You are the first person they see if anything goes wrong – so it is your fault!

Upstairs in the telephone enquiry office, Tracy Leach is one of a staff of five who answer about 1000 calls a day from the public. She goes home 'mentally exhausted'.

We get people ringing up from all over the place. Timetable enquiries aren't too bad but a lot of it is detective work. People always omit where they are going *from* because they think you know. You have to ask a lot of questions because of the different fares but a lot of people resent telling you.

Guards' duties

Responsibility for passengers does not worry Martin Kelly, who has been a guard at Rugby since 1969.

The driver is responsible for the engine but the guard is in charge of the train. If anything goes wrong we have to protect our passengers. We have to know where the signals are, where the telephones are – there is one about every mile along the track – and if the train fails we have to put down detonators so that a following driver will stop. Do they give a loud bang? Oh, yes – enough to wake him up!

Inside the train, he says, 'there is a lot more clerical work than there used to be. We have to check the tickets, issue excess fares and often issue tickets as well because some stations are not manned and passengers have to pay the guard.'

In a large bag Martin takes to the train the vast number of items required by a guard. They include: the *Rule Book*, which every railway worker has to have; a guard's instruction book; the train log-book; ticket examiner's handbook; fares manual; a passenger timetable; a working timetable; a book of excess fare tickets; ticket nippers; a padlock to lock mail and valuables in a cage in the brake van; green and red flags; twelve detonators; a carriage key for locking the doors if damage has been done inside; an orange High Visibility Vest, which everyone has to have for working on or near the track; and a special screwdriver in case anyone gets locked in the toilet. 'You have to be prepared for anything', he says.

Packed in beside all this he takes a mug and a small metal teapot with supplies of tea, milk and sugar.

If you have only ten minutes to turn around you can make a pot of tea in the messroom and bring it with you. You don't get a break and eight hours is a long time to go without a cup of tea.

Railway staff rooms have been called messrooms ever since the first companies were managed by military men. Each grade – drivers, guards, railmen – has its own messroom and nowadays all messrooms have facilities such as cookers, sinks and easy chairs. In many the staff have bought TV sets, fridges and sometimes microwave ovens and even fruit-machines.

Coping with 'bother'

Before becoming a guard at Waterloo in 1984, Deborah Walker spent three weeks at guards' training school where she had to pass written and practical tests and do a ticket course. She also had to learn 'route knowledge'. On the first day she 'worked' a train: 'I was like a bag of nerves, but once past a couple of stations, I was OK.' Now she enjoys the job because it means getting out and meeting people.

You do get a bit of bother sometimes, especially with drunks. They open the doors as the train is going along. I just say 'If you don't stop you'll be off at the next station.' They look at me as if to say 'Who does she think she's telling?' but they do stop. If it's really bad trouble you have to get on the telephone and have the police waiting.

I had a group of youngsters once who had been out fishing. I told them to stop throwing things out of the windows so they tipped all their maggots over the floor – they were crawling all over the passengers who got in. It was funny really but I made them clear them all up. A girl asked them why they'd done it and I heard them

45   *Deborah Walker tests the brake in the guards' van.*

say 'There's a miserable cow next door that's moaning.' I had to laugh at the end of it.

Equal opportunities

Deborah joined the railways as a carriage cleaner in 1982 and at that time there were only 42 women guards out of a total of nearly 12,000. By 1984 there were 59 guards, 34 women 'signalmen', two relief drivers and five driver's assistants, and 1,661 women 'railmen'. There were no women working on the permanent way. A report by the Equal Opportunities Commission in 1986 claimed that despite BR's policy of equal opportunities, there was still a great deal of prejudice against women by both management and staff. Job titles, such as 'signalman' and 'railman' had not been altered. Out of BR's total workforce of 170,000, 11,000 were women and most of these were in clerical jobs. Following the report, BR appointed an Equal Opportunities manager.

One thing Deborah hopes will change is the *Rule Book*, which she refers to as a 'Men Only' book. 'I'm not a great feminist but I do object to reading "he" all the time. By now they should have brought out one which says "persons" ', she says.

At work she finds

Most of the drivers are fine. I can have a laugh and joke with them. I reported one, though, because he was appalling. All he said to me was: 'You should not be doing this job. Women should be at home having babies.' I got on the phone and it ended with him getting a telling off.

Deborah has to operate the Red Star parcel scheme and do night newspaper loading – 'that soon builds up your muscles'. She works a 2.15 a.m. newspaper train which arrives back at Waterloo at 9.17 a.m. and 'by then you *are*

beginning to feel tired'. Nevertheless, she would recommend the job to any girl with the right personality.

You can still be feminine but you have got to be able to give and take. I go in the messroom and you can have a laugh. They don't expect me to make the tea all the time.

When Jenny Foster applied for the job of train recorder at Rugby power signalbox 'there was a certain amount of doubt about toilet facilities in the box. In the end I was allocated one to myself downstairs but I just use the one up here like the men. After all, its only like being at home.' Married to a builder, Jenny likes the shifts because they give her more time with her baby daughter than a nine to five job would do. She considers the railways 'pretty fair when it comes to women working with men. We are not segregated at all and they encourage us to get on.'

On each shift Rugby box has a supervisor, two signalmen, a train announcer and a train recorder, who is graded as a clerical officer and keeps a register of all train movements. 'The signalmen have been a great help', says Jenny. 'Each one has gone out of his way to explain it all to me. They know so much. To me, they are the cream on the cake.'

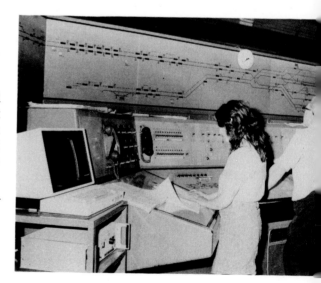

46 *Jenny Foster ventures into the signalmen's section to check an item under the track layout diagram at Rugby signalbox. Normally she sits at a desk behind the 'bobbies'.*

question of pressures and I suppose you get used to them in boxes but some people couldn't adapt.

At Hawkesbury Lane, near Bedworth, signalman Vic Walker does lone shifts in a manual box operated on the 'absolute block' system, in much the same way as his Victorian predecessors did. Vic has no desire to move to a power box. He says:

Here you are your own supervisor. You make your own decisions. I do get lonely but I like being alone. I am independent and the last thing I want is to be under too much pressure.

Signalmen have to be 'passed out' for each different box they work. Like other railway staff they receive specialized training at BR training schools.

Jobs on the railways, however, are scarce, especially in areas of high unemployment. Even in London both Paul and Deborah applied three times before they were accepted for training.

47 *At Hawkesbury Lane signalbox Vic Walker pulls the levers into 'reverse' in the same way as signalmen did 100 years ago.*

Signals

BR's Coventry area, which includes Rugby, has three power boxes and 15 manual ones. In power boxes signalmen direct drivers over long routes, changing signals and altering points by pressing buttons and turning switches. An electronic track-circuiting system, by which the passage of the train completes a circuit between the rails, means that along the line plotted by the 'bobby' on the track-layout diagram white lights turn to red as the train reaches them. The signalman has to regulate vast numbers of trains travelling to different places at different speeds. Electronic safety devices prevent him from mapping a route which would lead to a collision and in an emergency all signals automatically turn to red.

Derek Cornforth started his working life in a manual box and moved first to a miniature lever box and then to a power box at Darlington. He says:

You are enclosed in a power box: you don't see the trains as you did in an old manual box. It is a

Youth Training Scheme

In many areas junior employees are recruited from BR's Youth Training Scheme, which is run in conjunction with the Government Manpower Services Commission. John Brazier says: 'I rely a lot on YTS schemes now and usually recruit from them.'

Ticket inspector Ron Hooker, a railwayman since 1951, became YTS training co-ordinator in the Portsmouth Area when the scheme started in 1983. His 'school' is a cabin on platform 2 at Havant station. He says:

When I started there was no basic training but before they leave these lads will have had a basic training in all different aspects of railway work. This fallacy about young people not wanting to work is a load of rubbish. They do want to work but they want to see the end product. Here they are not used as cheap labour and they are not taking the place of other railway staff. They are always supervised.

BR has two courses – 'clerical' and 'traffic'. Trainees become members of the appropriate union on payment of a nominal subscription.

Mark Stones transferred to the clerical course after six months on traffic and on finishing in 1986 he got a job in the Area manager's office. He then became a clerical officer at Cosham.

I didn't want to go on a YTS but I couldn't get a job. People said things like: 'You're doing slave labour', or 'You can't be bothered to work' but BR's is one of the best courses in the area. I found

it enjoyable, we got valuable experience – and it did lead to a job for me. I think there is a pretty high success rate in the railways if you are ambitious. The opportunities are good.

Ian Hills was one of the 16 school-leavers who started on the course with Mark and he, too, had been reluctant to join. 'At first my friends were "taking the mick".' In 1987 he was working as a leading railman at Portsmouth and hoped, eventually, to be in charge of a one-man station. Although he has already been attacked by a passenger, he says: 'I'm not afraid of people attacking me. I can cope.'

Both agreed that abuse and vandalism were 'something you have got to live with'. Mark: 'At Cosham they close the waiting room early but the toilets get smashed and the slot-machines torn down.'

In Portsmouth all 12 who finished the course in 1986 managed to get jobs on BR, but in the North-East it was a different story. Of 37 who joined the Newcastle course in 1985, seven left, 11 got jobs on BR, 12 went on other courses or got jobs outside BR, and seven were still unemployed in late 1986.

One of those who failed to get a job on completing the course was Andrew Hall, who says:

48 *Former YTS trainee Ian Hills. In 1987 he was working as a leading railman at Portsmouth and hoped, eventually, to be in charge of a one-man station.*

I want to work on BR. I always have done. At school I was always saying I wanted something on BR but the careers master said 'We've never had anyone go to British Rail.' I kept going back and nagging them and in the end they sent for some leaflets. On the YTS we get a good view of what happens on the railway. I have worked in the parcels office, as a travelling cleaner on the trains, in the office at Gateshead shed, on the computer, in the engineers' department, and I got a chance to paint one of the locos when the Queen Mother came up.

At the moment there are few applications for the BR scheme from girls. Jill Male, however, joined the same course as Andrew. On her first day:

49 *YTS trainees on the 1985-6 course at Newcastle. Jill Male is in front and Andrew Hall stands behind her.*

I walked into the room. There were 22 desks. One was mine and all the rest were filled with lads. I thought 'Help!' At first it was 'Jill's a lass, she'll make the coffee' but I told them: 'Just because I'm a lass it doesn't mean I have to do it. I came on the course to be treated like you are.' It was alright after a few days. I've got some good friends now. I have really enjoyed it and I have not found any prejudice from anyone on BR.

After their on-the-job basic training the trainees could choose to learn more about one particular job. Jill chose catering and worked in the buffet at York station. On leaving she got a place on a catering course at a technical college.

The future

Young trainees today join a railway which is very different from the one their predecessors worked on a hundred years ago, at the height of the Victorian age of industrial prosperity.

Then, railway companies, which commanded the transport network, preached expansion; BR's policy, in an era of industrial decline, stresses economy. Gone are the hotels and the Sealink services; many of the station catering outlets are in private hands. Workshop redundancies caused a storm in the mid-80s, especially when the historic Swindon works was closed down.

Though working conditions have steadily improved since the nineteenth and early twentieth centuries, the number of railway workers has relentlessly fallen. In 1986 cuts in Government funding caused railwaymen further fears for the future of jobs and services. Many regarded proposals for the 'privatization' of nationalized industries, such as BR, as an additional threat.

Colin Forster is able to say: 'They always called railways "A job for life", and for me it has proved to be so.' But a younger colleague, Bill Mack, who became a driver in 1985, wonders: 'Will there be a job for me in the future? I am pessimistic.'

Harry Lofkin speaks for many when he says: 'Engineers should run the railways, not accountants; safety should come top of the list, not cost.' Nevertheless, he adds: 'I think there is still some scope on the P-way today. I would still recommend it as a job.'

The railway which runs into the twenty-first century will be very much a streamlined version of the system which started when *Locomotion*

50 *Electra is intended to be Inter City's flagship locomotive of the 1990s and will be used on the east coast main line between Kings Cross and Edinburgh when it is electrified.*

---

puffed and rattled along the rails to Stockton. On provincial routes new diesels called Sprinters and Pacers have now replaced elderly DMUs; on main lines HSTs will give way to 140 m.p.h. Electra locomotives hauling tilting carriages to take the bends. Electrification of the east coast main line, down which the *Flying Scotsman* and *Mallard* pounded on their record-breaking runs, will be complete by the early 1990s. In 1987 plans for a Channel Tunnel rail link with France were taking shape.

Freight yards all over the country are linked by computer to a Total Operations Processing System (TOPS) in London, and computers play their part in all aspects of modern railway organization from booking office to signalbox. As new advances are made through developments such as microprocessing, railway jobs will inevitably become more and more specialized.

'Railway family'

Amid all the changes, however, one factor remains constant. Time and again railway workers speak of the 'family feeling' on the railways. This is there not only because of the tradition of 'railway families' but, more importantly, because railway jobs, though so diverse, are interdependent. Safety factors alone dictate that, just like the signalling system itself, they must interlock, one with the other.

Paul James, on the threshold of his career, gives his view of railway life:

Driving is a skilled job. It is like being an engineer. You have to work pretty hard, but I enjoy the people. We must have the funniest people in the whole of England. It is not just Waterloo drivers; the drivers who come from Salisbury are just as jolly. Everyone takes it as one happy family.

As modern technology sends faster trains speeding into the future, let us hope that this family spirit will not be left behind.

Abbreviations

ASLEF Associated Society of Locomotive Engineers and Firemen
ASRS Amalgamated Society of Railway Servants
BR British Railways or, from 1964, British Rail
GER Great Eastern Railway
GNR Great Northern Railway
GWR Great Western Railway
LB & SCR London, Brighton & South Coast Railway

LDC Local Departmental Committee
LMSR London, Midland & Scottish Railway
LNER London & North Eastern Railway
LNWR London & North Western Railway
NER North Eastern Railway
NUR National Union of Railwaymen
S & DR Stockton and Darlington Railway
SR Southern Railway
TSSA Transport Salaried Staff's Association

Date List

1825	Opening of Stockton & Darlington Railway
1829	Rainhill Trials
1830	Liverpool & Manchester Railway opened
1836-50	'Railway Mania'
1844	Gladstone's Railway Act – 1d a mile
1861	Clayton Tunnel collision
1871	ASRS formed
1877	Royal Commission on Railway Accidents
1879	First Pullman car introduced, on GNR
1879	Tay Bridge disaster
1880	ASLEF formed
1897	Railway Clerks' Association formed
1900	Taff Vale case
1911	First national railway strike
1913	Three unions amalgamate to form NUR
1914-18	First World War
1919	National railway strike
1923	Railway 'grouping'
1926	General Strike
1939-45	Second World War
1948	Nationalization of the railways
1955	ASLEF strike and Guillebaud Report
1960	Last steam engine built
1963	Beeching Report
1966	Penzance Agreement
1968	BREL set up as separate company
1973	HSTs put into service
1982	Strikes over BR's new proposals, including flexible rostering
1986	Cuts in Government funding and closure of Swindon engineering works

Glossary

amalgamate join together

anarchist a person who believes in a political philosophy which advocates the destruction of government

benefits sums of money paid in place of wages to workers who are sick or unemployed. Benefit societies were set up to pay such allowances to their members; trade unions give strike benefit to members out on strike.

Box Brownie one of the first mass-produced cameras, simple to use and cheap to buy

blackleg someone who continues in employment while his fellow workers are on strike

branch lines smaller railway lines running off the main routes

damages sums of money awarded by courts in compensation for loss or injury

Depression, The term used to describe the social and economic conditions, especially in the 1920s and 1930s, when industries closed and many people were unemployed

detonators cylinders filled with explosive for use as warning devices on the track, especially in fog

footplate the platform on which the driver and fireman stand in a steam locomotive cab

firebox the part of a steam engine which contains the fire. The fireman shovels coal into it through a door opening from the cab.

flexible rostering a system of shifts in which starting and finishing times can be varied

freight merchandise and property moved by rail, also known as goods

gauge the width between rails

hard labour a prison sentence under which the prisoner has to work at arduous tasks such as breaking rocks

humanitarian concerned with human welfare

injector device for directing water into a steam engine's boiler

letters of administration legal authority to deal with the estate, or property, of someone who has died

marshalling yards railway lines laid out for the purpose of assembling goods trains

manslaughter legal term used when a death or deaths result from actions, such as carelessness, by another person but where there is no intention to kill, as there is in murder

monopoly sole right to trade or run an organization such as a business or service

meticulous giving careful attention to detail

munitions war weapons such as guns and ammunition

percentage disability assessment of the extent of an injury or other disablement for which a reduced benefit sum is paid

pick-up goods a train that stops at different stations along a line to collect or deliver goods

points movable sections of rail which can be switched to transfer trains from one line to another

Royal Commision a body of people appointed by the Government to investigate and report on a particular problem

redundancy dismissal from work of employees no longer needed, usually because of cuts or closures

semaphore system of signalling by means of movable arms or arrangements of lanterns or flags

sand boxes containers for sand, which was dropped on the rails to stop locomotive wheels from slipping

shunter engine driver who moves trucks in marshalling yards or goods sidings

smokebox front section of a steam locomotive where the smoke collects before coming out of the funnel

second man co-driver or assistant driver on

diesel or electric trains. The second man on
steam engines was the fireman.

single-manning system whereby a train has only
one driver with no co-driver or assistant in the
cab

superannuation pension, usually paid on
retirement

viaduct structure built to carry a railway line
over an expanse of land such as a valley, as a
bridge does over water

Books for Further Reading

Books about railway workers

Philip S. Bagwell, *The Railwaymen* (history of the
NUR), George Allen & Unwin, 2 vols, 1963 and
1982
Terry Coleman, *The Railway Navvies*, Pelican
Books, 1968
Wilson Cornforth, *The Long Hard Road*,
D. Cornforth, 1985
John Farrington, *Life on the Lines*, Moorland
Publishing, 1984
Sir Francis Head, *Stokers and Pokers*, first
published 1855; reprinted by Frank Cass & Co,
1968
Jim Hill, *Buckjumpers, Gobblers and Clauds*,
D. Bradford Barton Ltd, 1981 (several other books
of railway reminiscences are in the same series)
Hugh Jenkins, *Working with British Rail*, Batsford,
1984
R.S. Joby, *The Railwaymen*, David & Charles,
1984
Rowland Kenney, *Men and Rails*, T. Fisher
Unwin, 1913
P.W. Kingsford, *Victorian Railwaymen*, Frank
Cass & Co., 1970
Frank McKenna, *The Railway Workers 1840-
1970*, Faber & Faber, 1980
Norman McKillop, *The Lighted Flame* (history of
ASLEF), Thomas Nelson, 1950
Rosemary Manning, *Railways and Railwaymen*,
Kestrel Books, 1977
P. Ransome-Wallis, ed., *Men of the Footplate*, Ian
Allan Ltd, 1954

J.R. Raynes, *Engines and Men* (history of ASLEF),
Goodhall & Suddick, 1921
Michael Reynolds, *Engine-Driving Life*, first
published 1881; reprinted by Hugh Evelyn Ltd,
1968
Ernest J. Simmons, *Memoirs of a Station Master*,
first published anonymously as *Ernest Struggles*
in 1897; reprinted by Adams & Dart, 1974

Railway histories

Michael Bowler, *The Official British Rail Book of
Trains for Young People*, Hutchinson, 1985
R.A.S. Hennessey, *Railways*, Batsford, 1973
Michael Robbins, *The Railway Age*, Penguin,
1970

Three nineteenth-century 'classics':
Sir William Acworth, *The Railways of England*,
John Murray, 1891
G.A. Sekon, *A History of the Great Western
Railway*, Digby Long, 1895
F.S. Williams, *Our Iron Roads*, Ingram Cooke,
1852; reprinted 1888

Other books of interest

Philippa Bignell, *Taking the Train*, HMSO for the
National Railway Museum
Hunter Davies, *George Stephenson*, Quartet
Books, 1977

O.S. Nock, *The Railway Engineers*, Batsford, 1955; *Historic Railway Disasters*, Arrow, 1970
L.T.C. Rolt, *Isambard Kingdom Brunel*, Longman, 1957; *George and Robert Stephenson*, Longman, 1960; *Red for Danger*, Pan, 1966

E. Nesbit's novel, *The Railway Children*, written in 1906, has been reprinted by Puffin Books and made into both a TV series and a film.

Places to Visit

Beamish North of England Open Air Museum, Stanley, Co. Durham. Working exhibits include Rowley Station, removed from its site when the branch line was closed in 1966 and reconstructed here with signal box, goods yard and steam trains.

Darlington Railway Museum, housed in the old North Road Station and home of the original *Locomotion*.

Great Western Railway Museum, Swindon, Wilts. Exhibits illustrate the history of the GWR and there is also a turn-of-the-century foreman's house in the GWR's railway village.

National Museum of Labour History, Old Limehouse Town Hall, Commercial Road, London E14. Exhibits on 'labour landmarks' such as the General Strike, and a good collection of trade union banners, including those of ASLEF, the ASRS and the NUR.

National Railway Museum, Leeman Road, York. Vast national collection of railway exhibits, ranging from locomotives such as *Mallard* down to uniforms, timetables and tickets.

Science Museum, Exhibition Road, London SW7. Exhibits, including Stephenson's *Rocket*, to illustrate engineering and transport history.

Steamtown Railway Museum, Carnforth, Lancashire. The home, among other exhibits, of the *Flying Scotsman*.

There are many more railway and transport museums around the country and, in addition, most railway preservation societies, such as the Buckinghamshire Railway Centre near Aylesbury and the Scottish Railway Preservation Society at Falkirk, are open at weekends and also hold regular 'steaming days'.

Index

Numbers in bold refer to pages on which illustrations occur.